Master Perfect Handwriting Workbook
Learn to Trace~Draw~Write

This Book Belongs to:

Name: _______________________

Class: _______________________

Legal & Disclaimer
The information contained in this book and its contents is not designed to replace or take the place of any form of medical or professional advice; and is not meant to replace the need for independent medical, financial, legal or other professional advice or services, as may be required. The content and information in this book has been provided for educational and entertainment purposes only.

The content and information contained in this book has been compiled from sources deemed reliable, and it is accurate to the best of the Author's knowledge, information and belief. However, the Author cannot guarantee its accuracy and validity and cannot be held liable for any errors and/or omissions. Further, changes are periodically made to this book as and when needed. Where appropriate and/or necessary, you must consult a professional (including but not limited to your doctor, attorney, financial advisor or such other professional advisor) before using any of the suggested remedies, techniques, or information in this book.

Upon using the contents and information contained in this book, you agree to hold harmless the Author from and against any damages, costs, and expenses, including any legal fees potentially resulting from the application of any of the information provided by this book. This disclaimer applies to any loss, damages or injury caused by the use and application, whether directly or indirectly, of any advice or information presented, whether for breach of contract, tort, negligence, personal injury, criminal intent, or under any other cause of action.

You agree to accept all risks of using the information presented inside this book.

You agree that by continuing to read this book, where appropriate and/or necessary, you shall consult a professional (including but not limited to your doctor, attorney, or financial advisor or such other advisor as needed) before using any of the suggested remedies, techniques, or information in this book.

Table of Contents

Introduction

The exercises in this book are specially for children or whoever wants to practice and improve handwriting plus drawing skills.

This book is equipped with 4 sections. Difficulty will increase gradually starting from Tracing Lines next to Drawing Shapes, Writing Alphabets and finally Writing Numbers.

There are ample spaces for you to practice and perfect handwriting and drawing skills.

Get Ready your Writing Materials: Pencil, Pen or Color pencils!

Enjoy the fun and look forward to other Master Perfect Handwriting Workbook.

Start Tracing the Lines

Straight Line

Sample:

Start Tracing Straight Line:

Mountain Line

Sample:

Start Tracing Mountain Line:

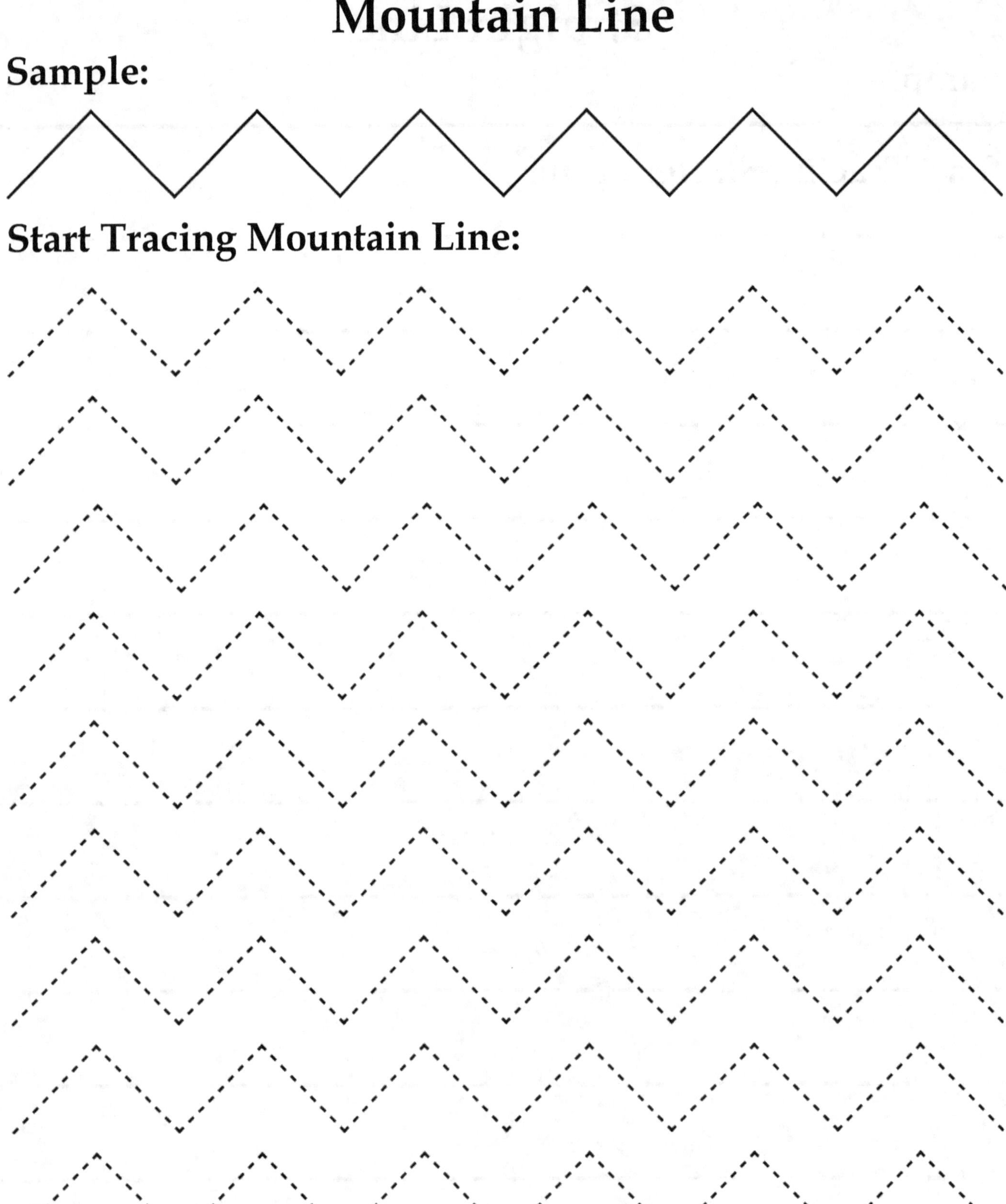

Zig-Zag Line

Sample:

Start Tracing Zig-Zag Line:

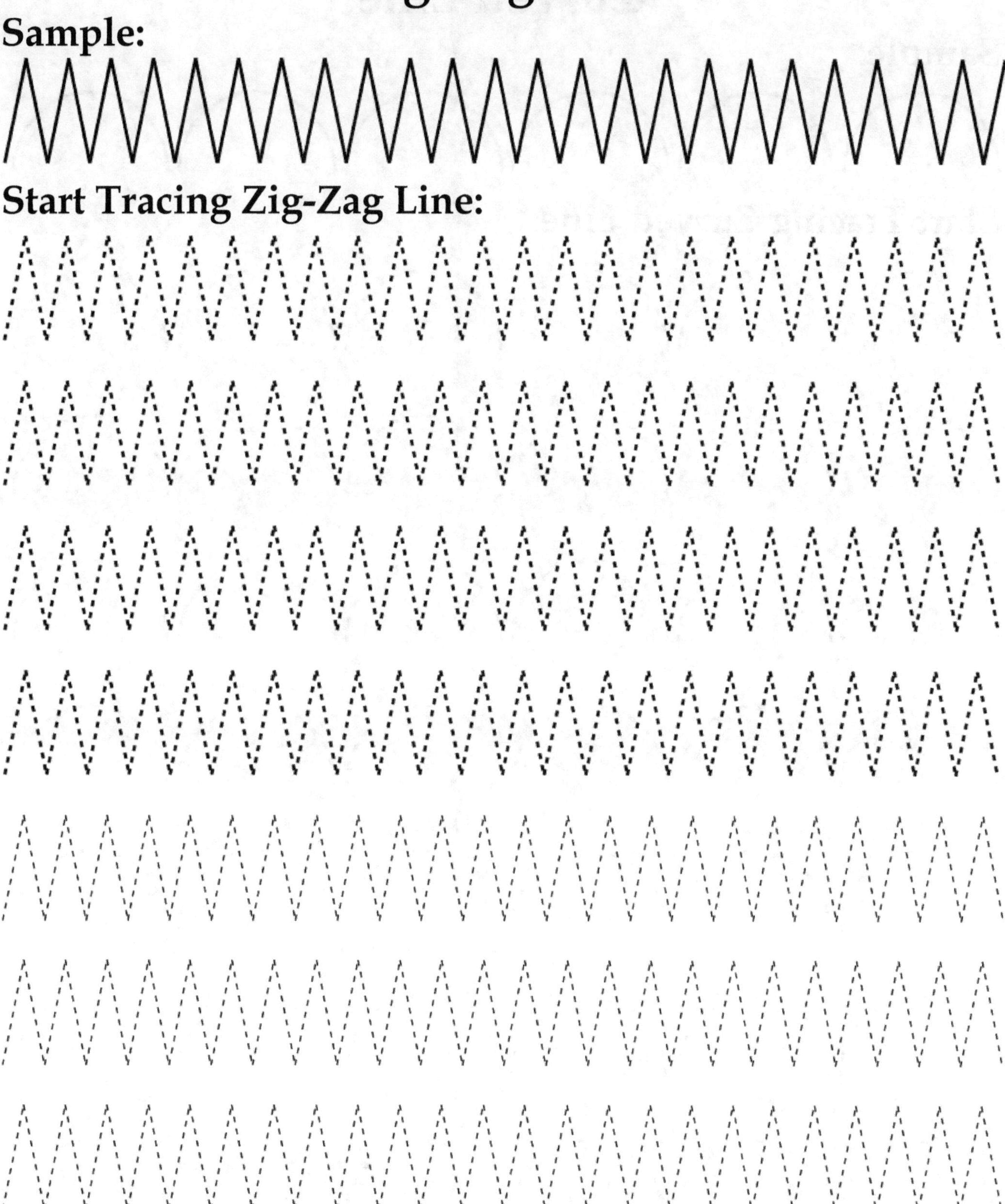

Curved Line

Sample:

Start Tracing Curved Line:

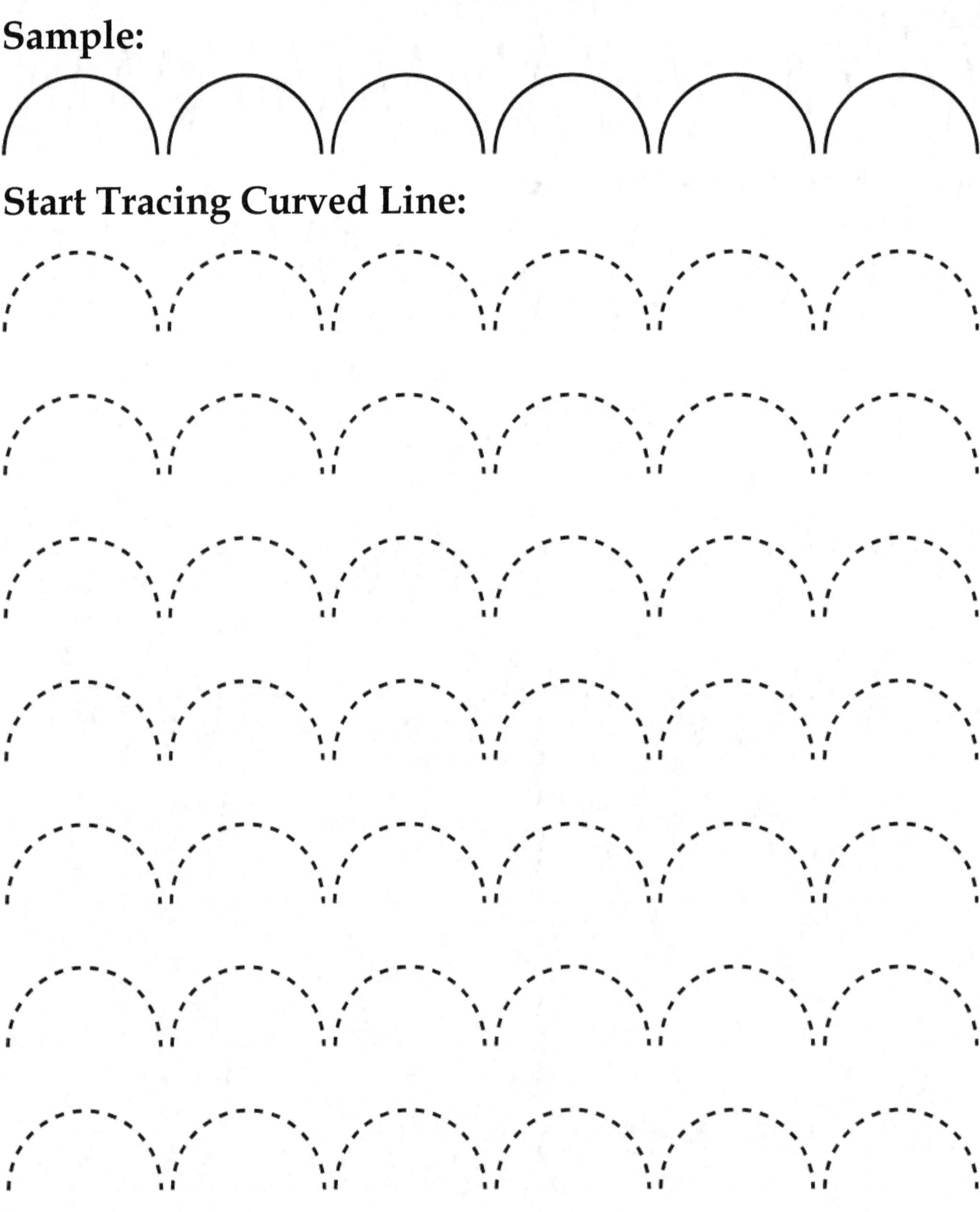

Wavy Line

Sample:

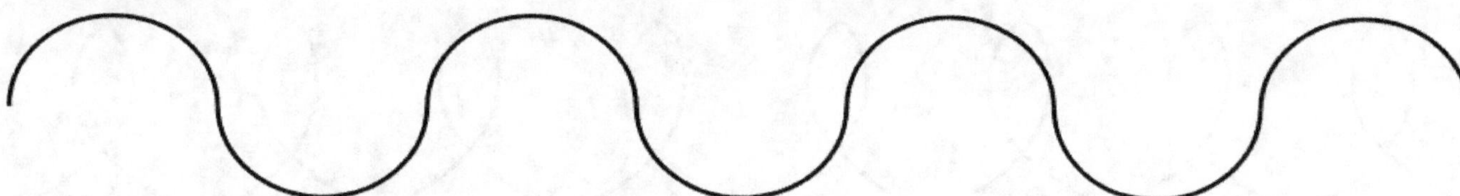

Start Tracing Wavy Line:

Loop-D-Loop Line

Sample:

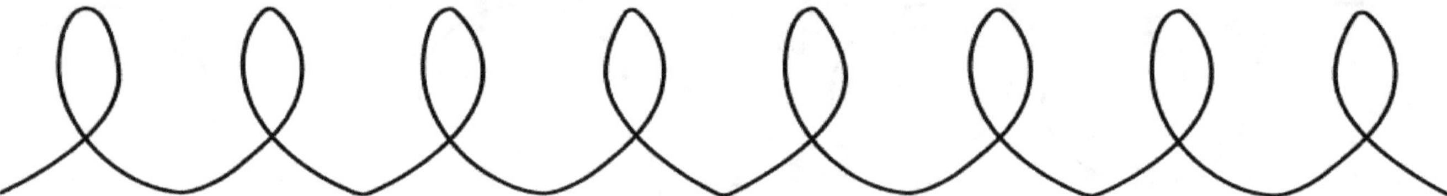

Start Tracing Loop-D-Loop Line:

Spiral Line

Sample:

Start Tracing Spiral Line:

Start Drawing Shapes

Triangle

Follow the lines to draw Triangle:

Square

Follow the lines to draw Square:

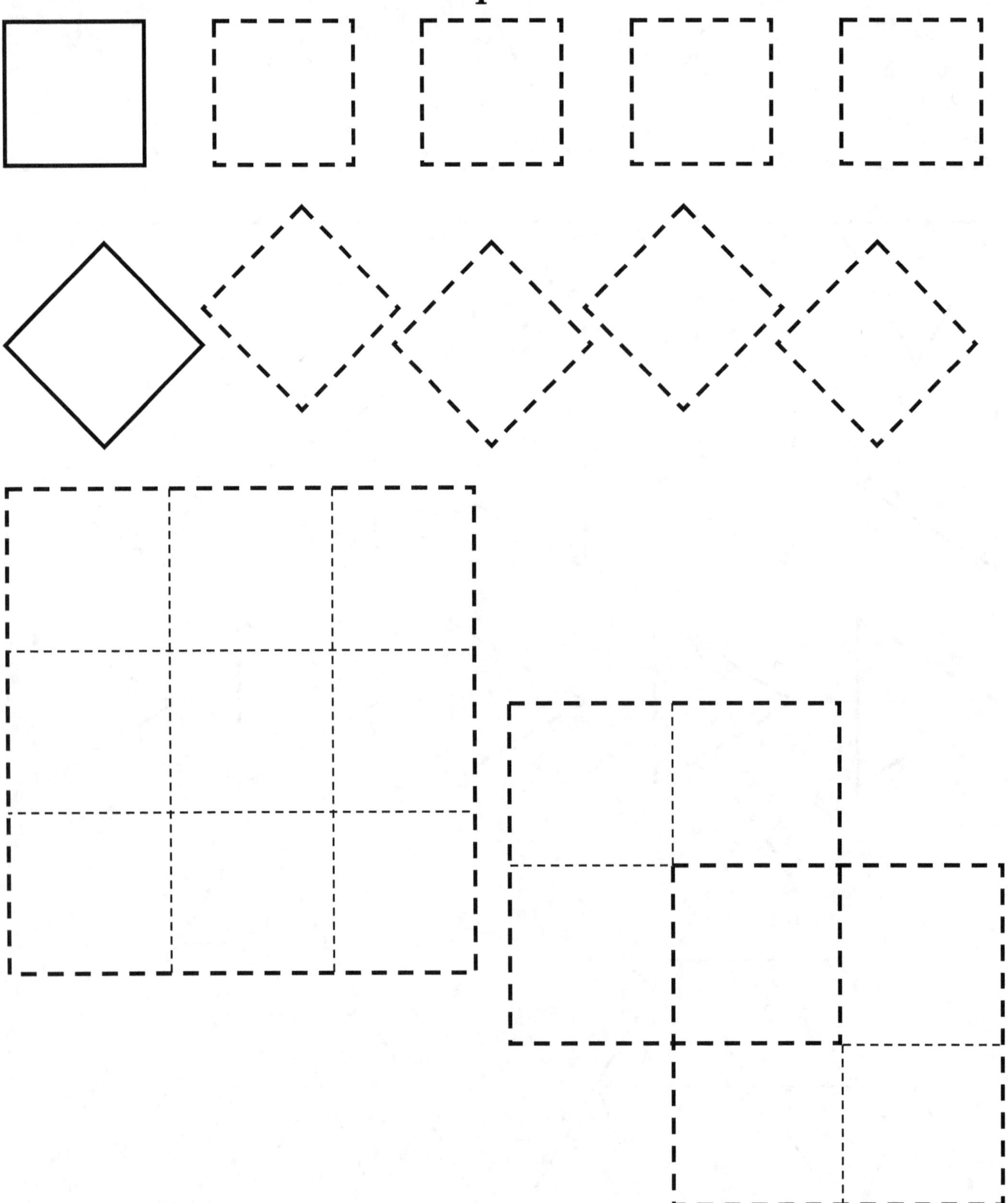

Pentagon

Follow the lines to draw Pentagon:

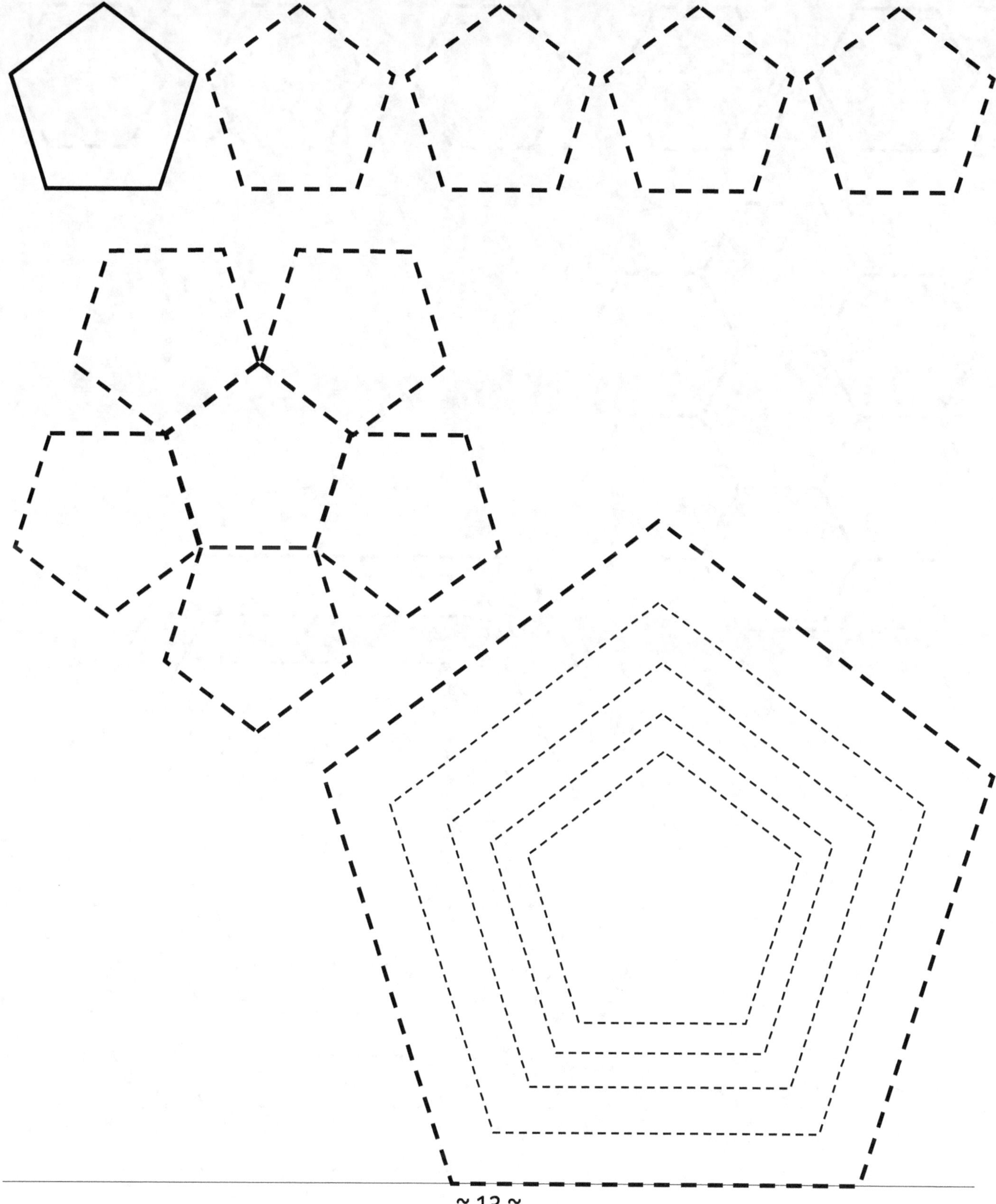

Hexagon

Follow the lines to draw Hexagon:

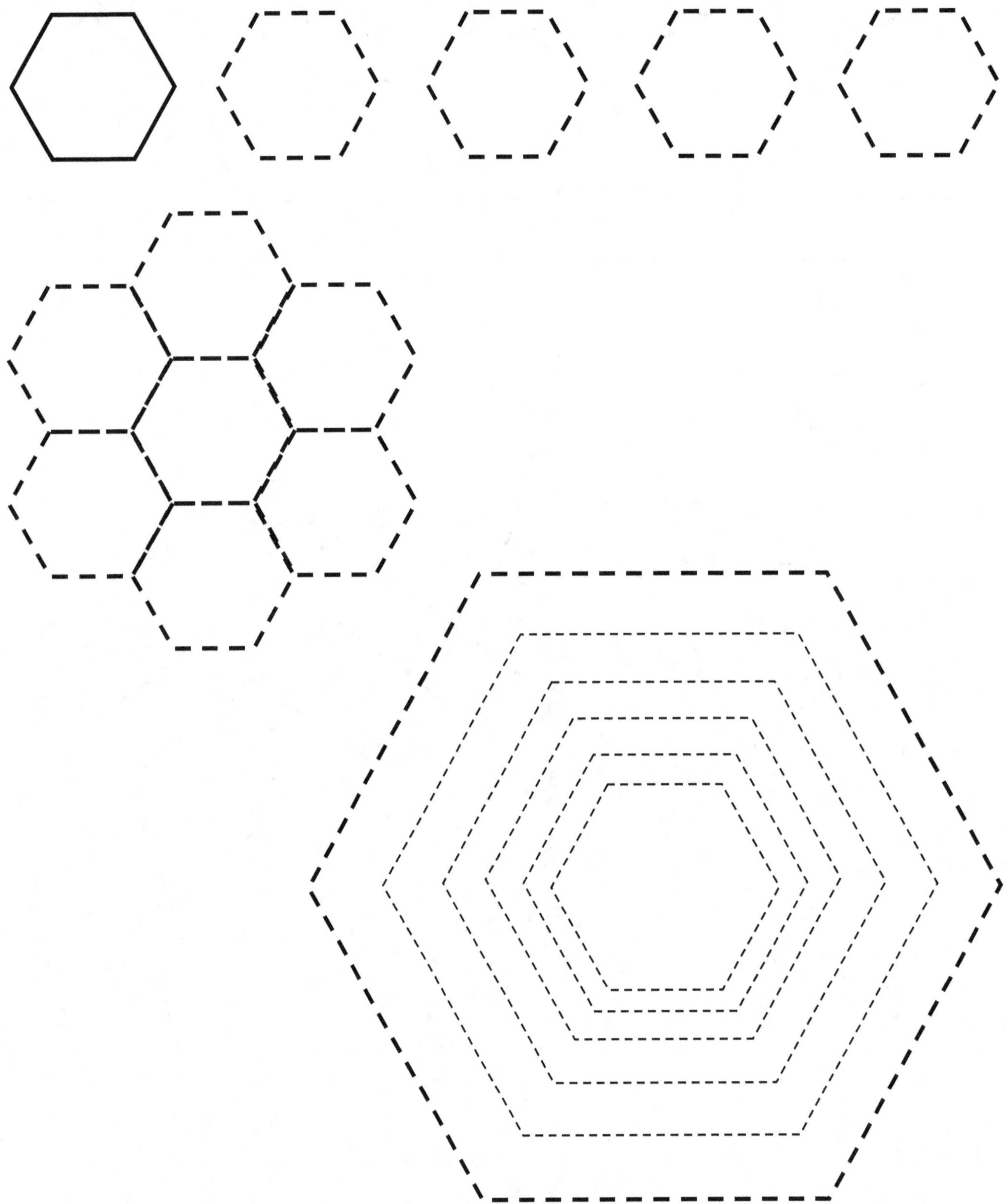

Star

Follow the lines to draw Star:

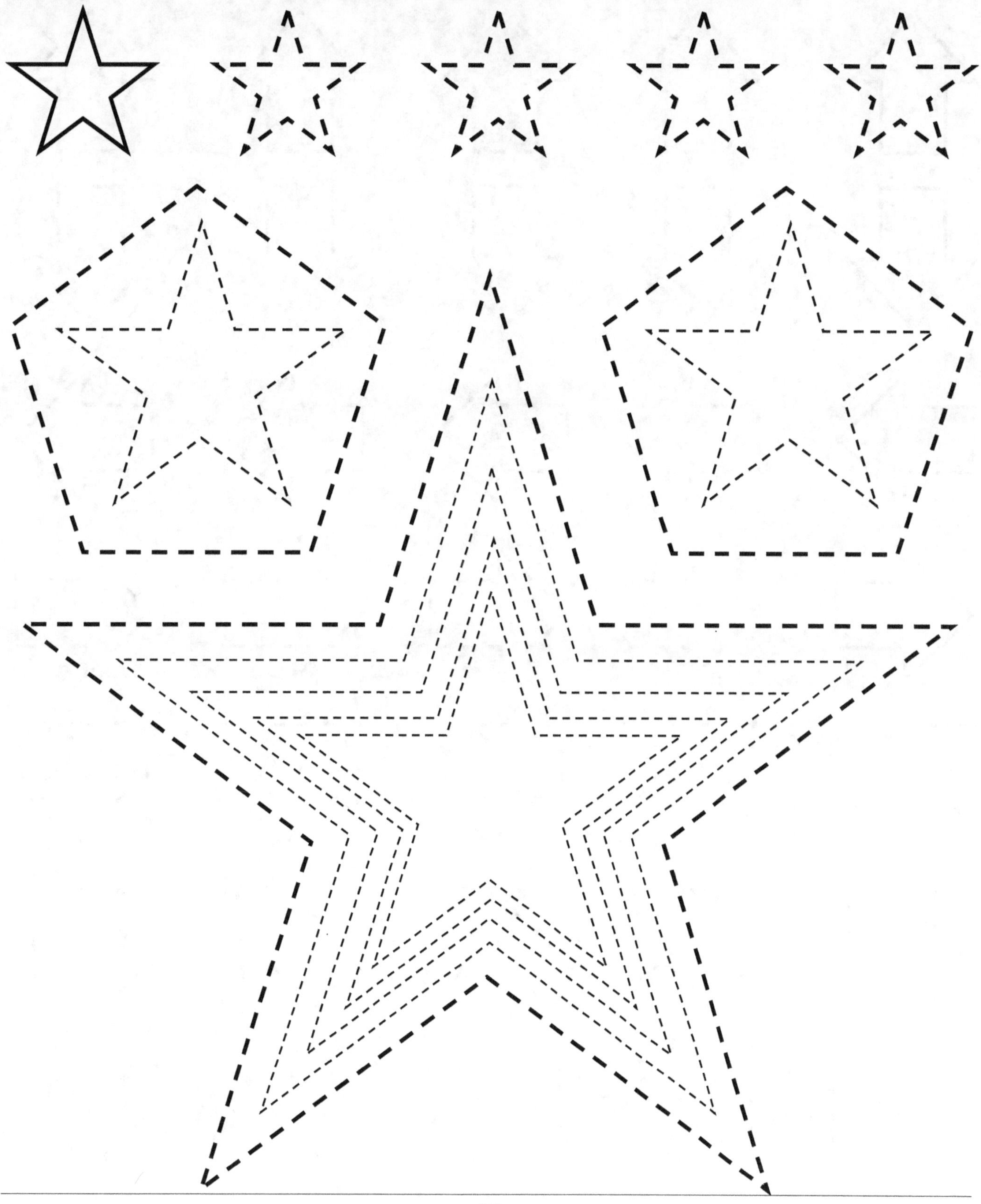

Arrow

Follow the lines to draw Arrow:

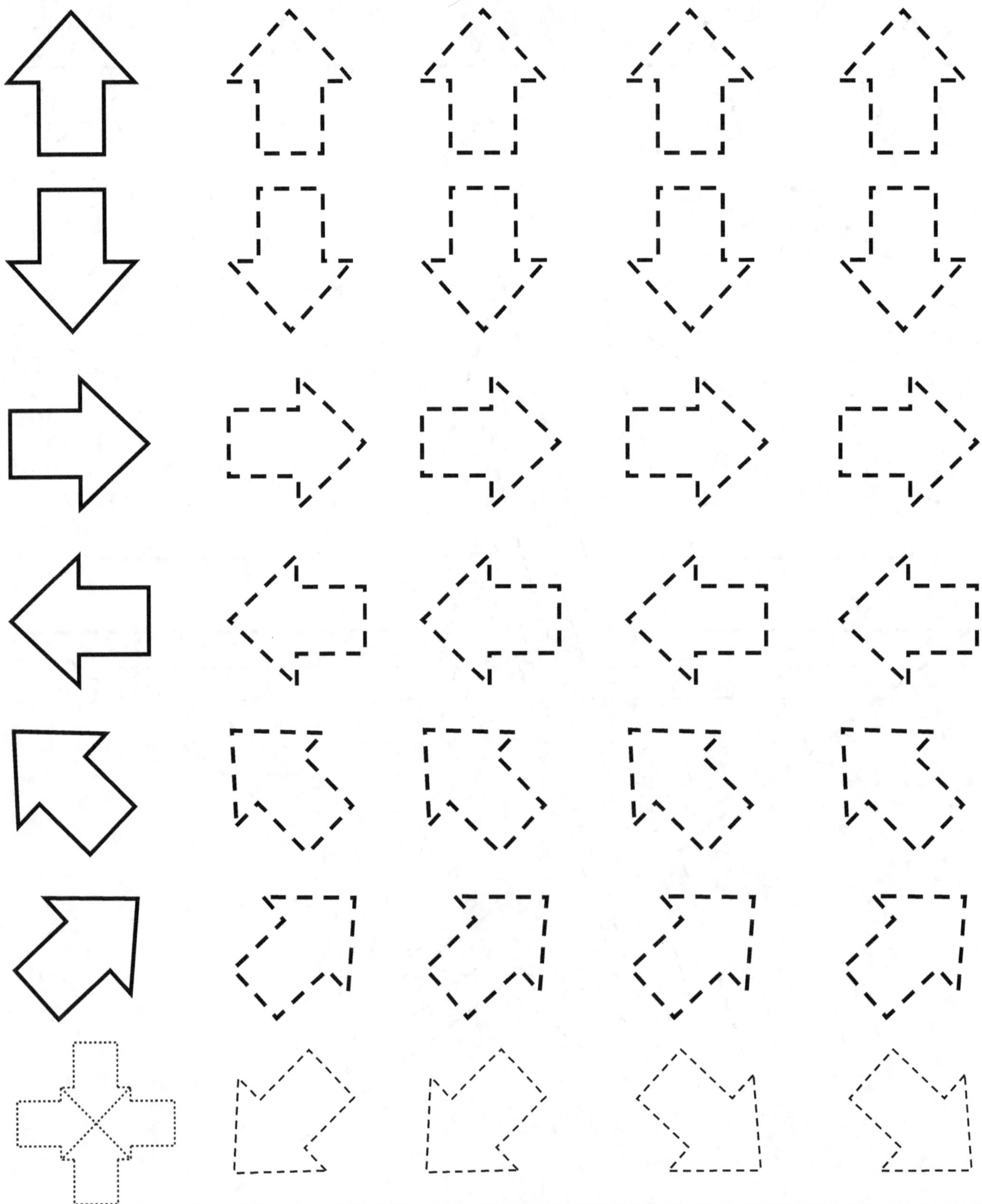

Cube

Follow the lines to draw Cube:

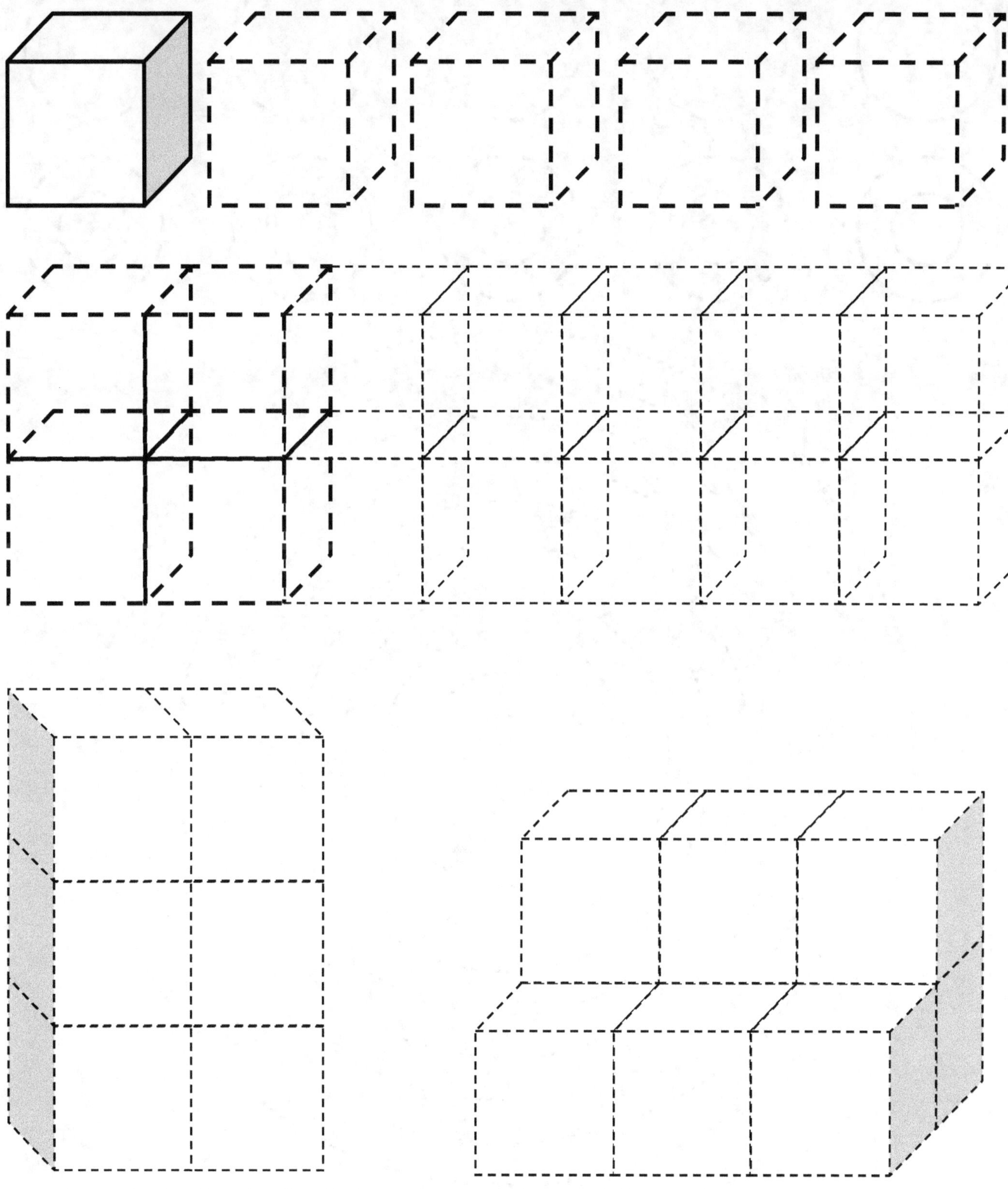

Circle

Follow the lines to draw Circle:

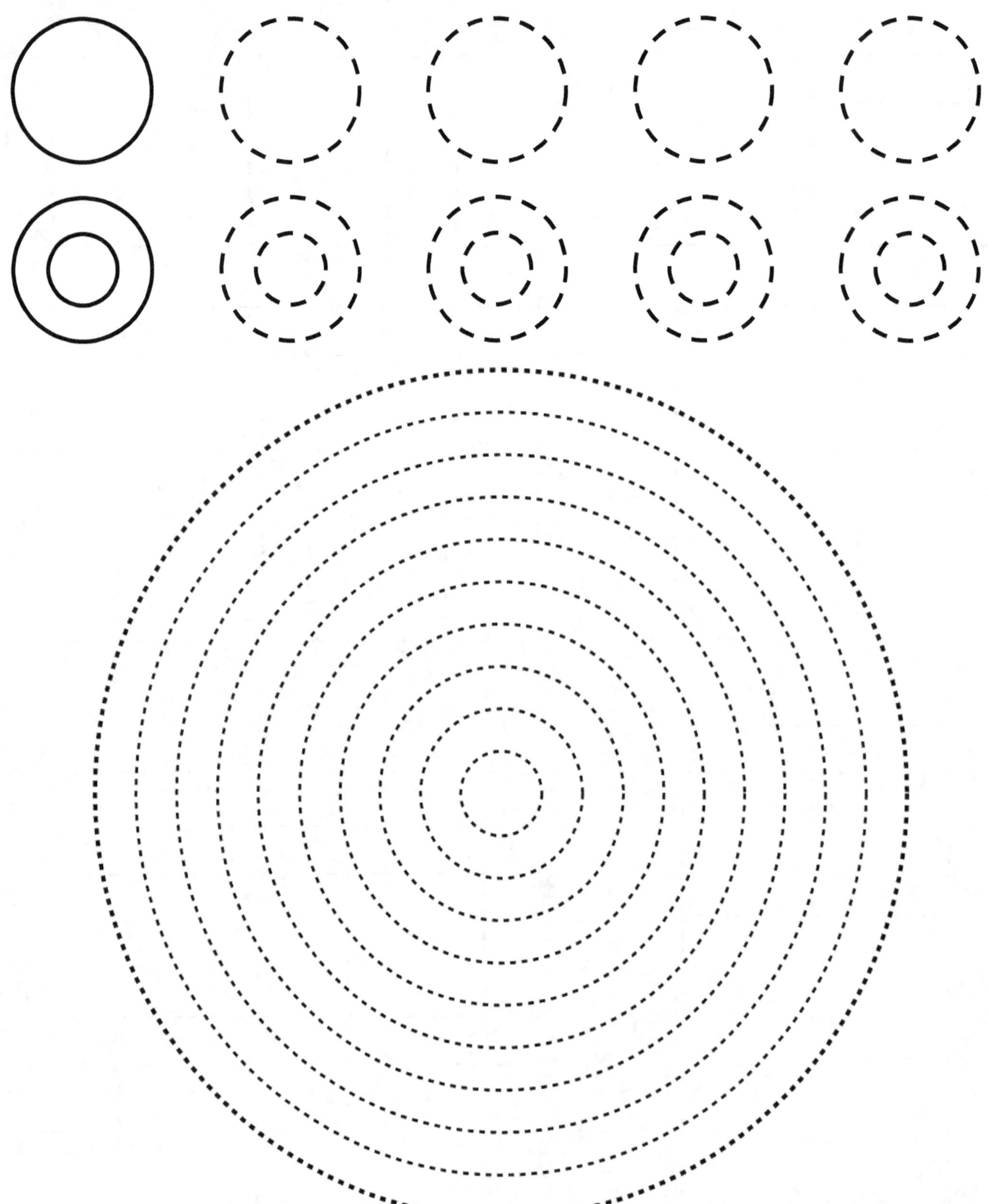

Oval

Follow the lines to draw Oval:

Moon

Follow the lines to draw Moon:

Smiley Face

Follow the lines to draw Smiley Face:

Heart

Follow the lines to draw Heart:

Sun

Follow the lines to draw Sun:

Start Writing Alphabets A-Z

Aa

Follow the dots to write Aa:

Words starting with the letter A:

→ Alligator – Alligator is a dangerous reptile.
→ Amusing – I find this cartoon amusing.
→ Australia – Australia is a country.

Bb

Follow the dots to write Bb:

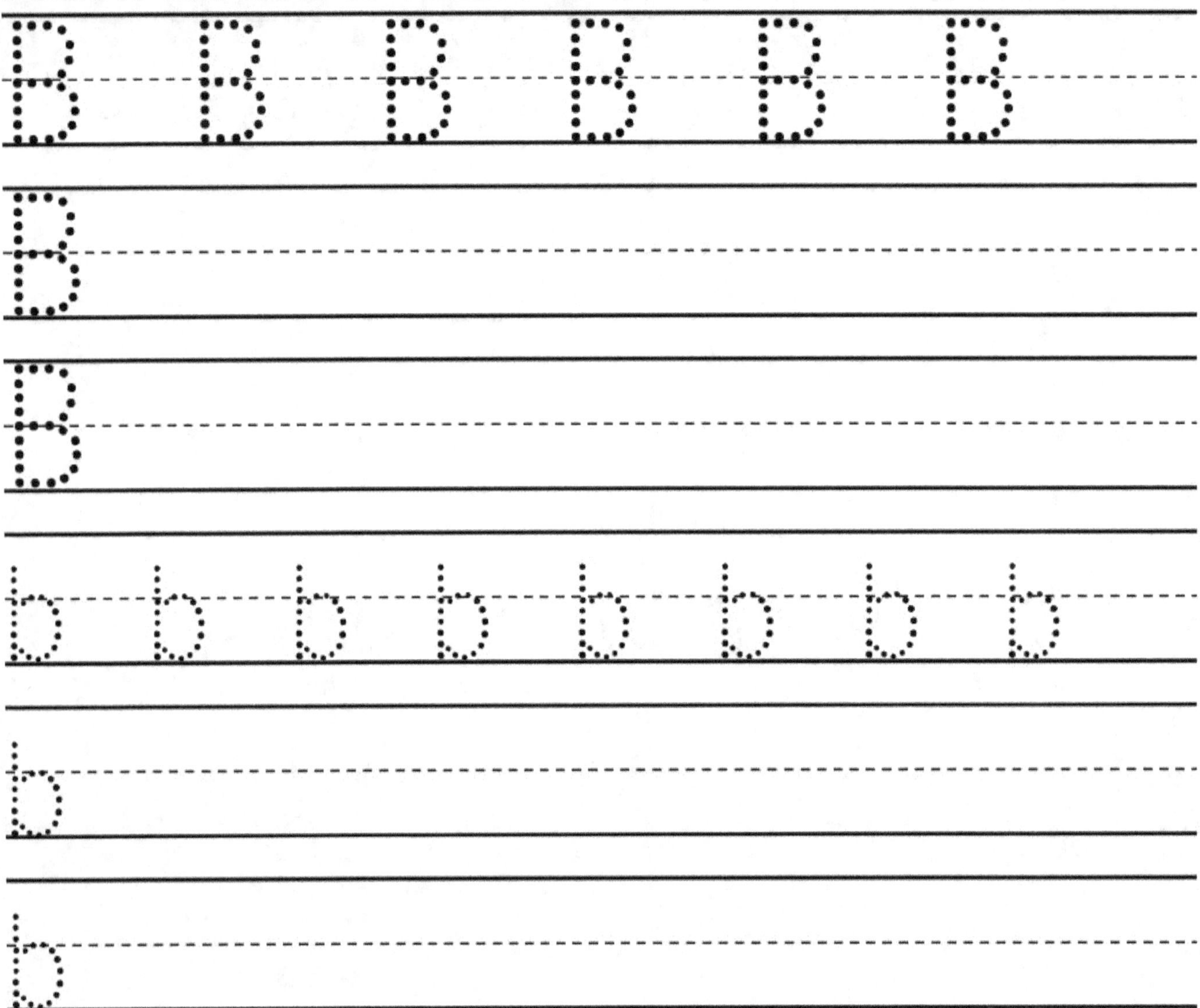

Words starting with the letter B:

→ Baboon – Baboon is a primate.
→ Boring – This comedy show is boring.
→ Belgium – Belgium is a country.

Cc

Follow the dots to write Cc:

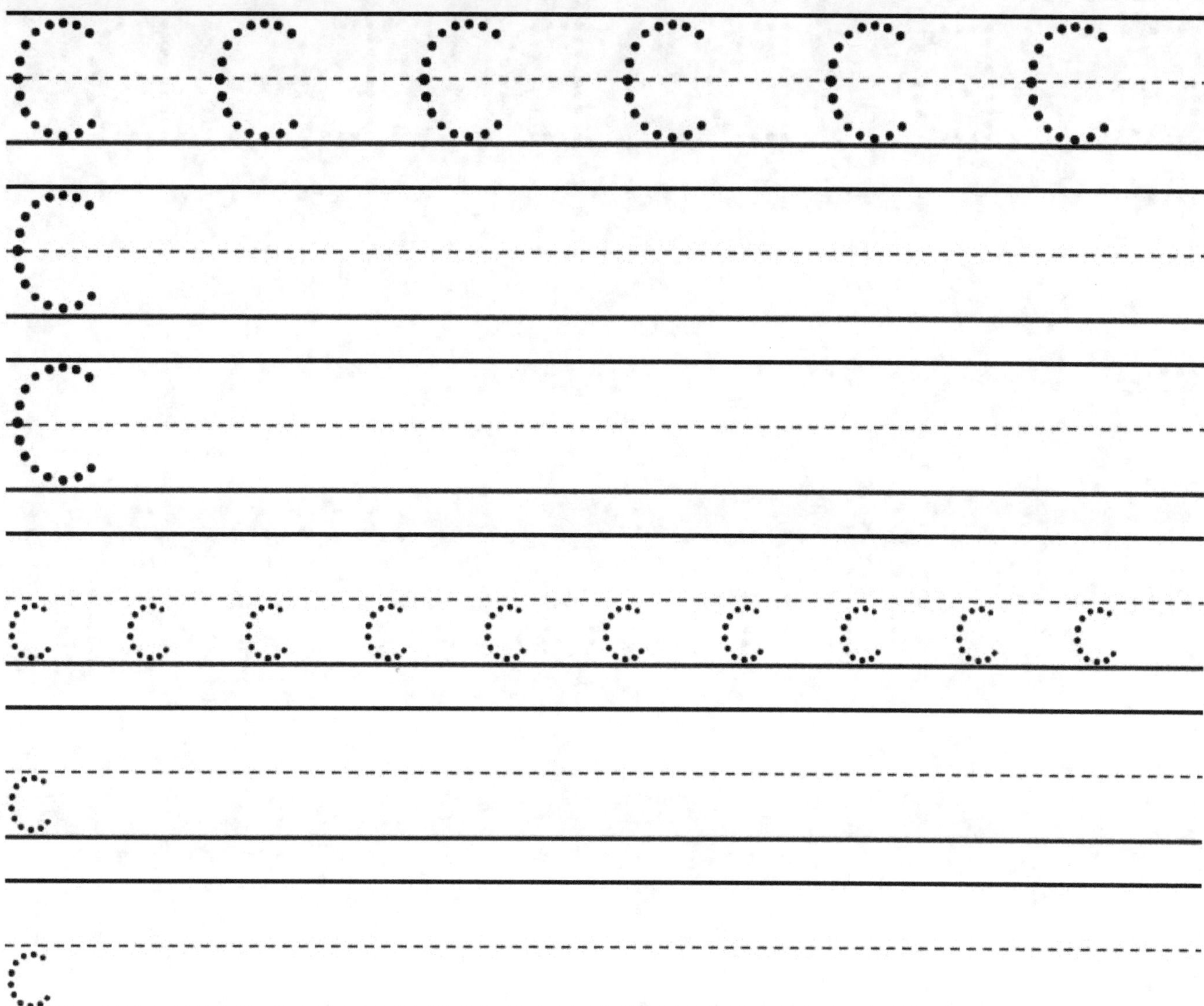

Words starting with the letter C:

➔ Cat – My pet is a cat.
➔ Curious – I'm curious how magic works.
➔ China – China is a country.

Dd

Follow the dots to write Dd:

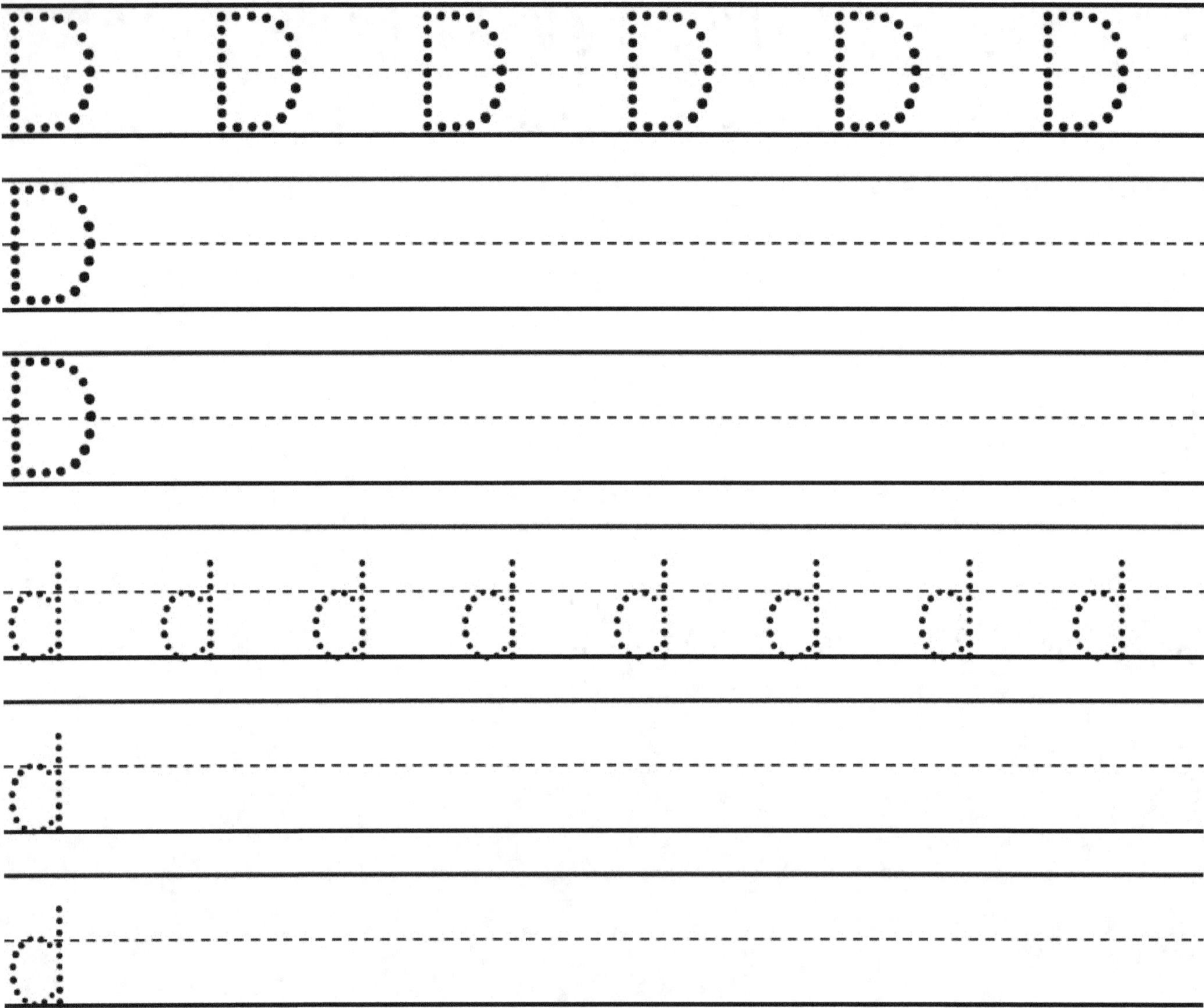

Words starting with the letter D:

- → Dog – My pet is a dog.
- → Delicious – My mom cooks delicious meals.
- → Denmark – Denmark is a country

Ee

Follow the dots to write Ee:

Words starting with the letter E:

→ Eagle – Eagle is a bird.
→ Eager – I'm eager to go for holiday.
→ Egypt – Egypt is a country.

Ff

Follow the dots to write Ff:

Words starting with the letter F:

➜ Fish – Fish lives in the water.
➜ Fun – I had fun in the amusement park.
➜ Finland - Finland is a country.

Gg

Follow the dots to write Gg:

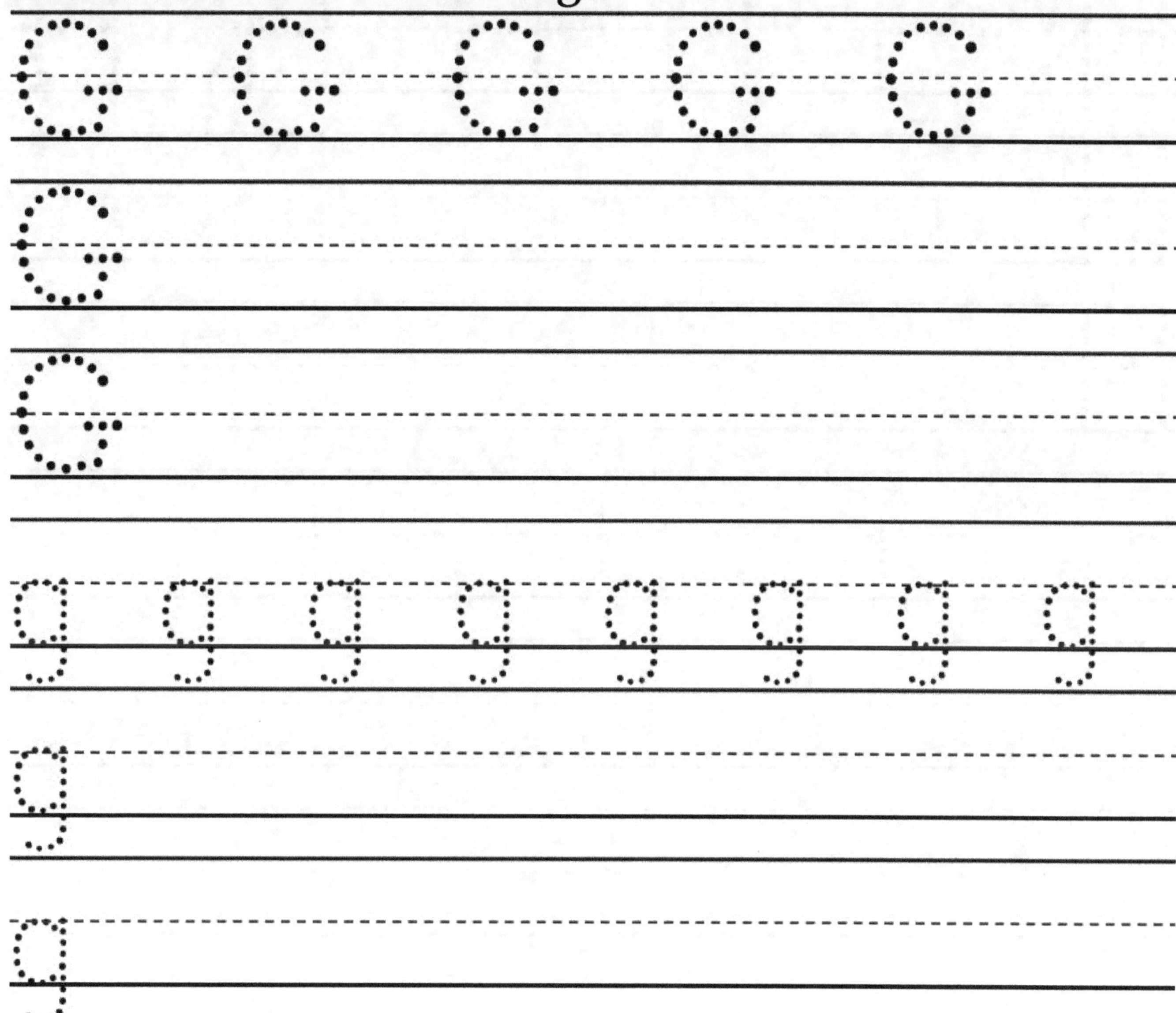

Words starting with the letter G:

➔ Goldfish – My pet is a goldfish.
➔ Grateful – I'm grateful with my teacher.
➔ Ghana – Ghana is a country.

Hh

Follow the dots to write Hh:

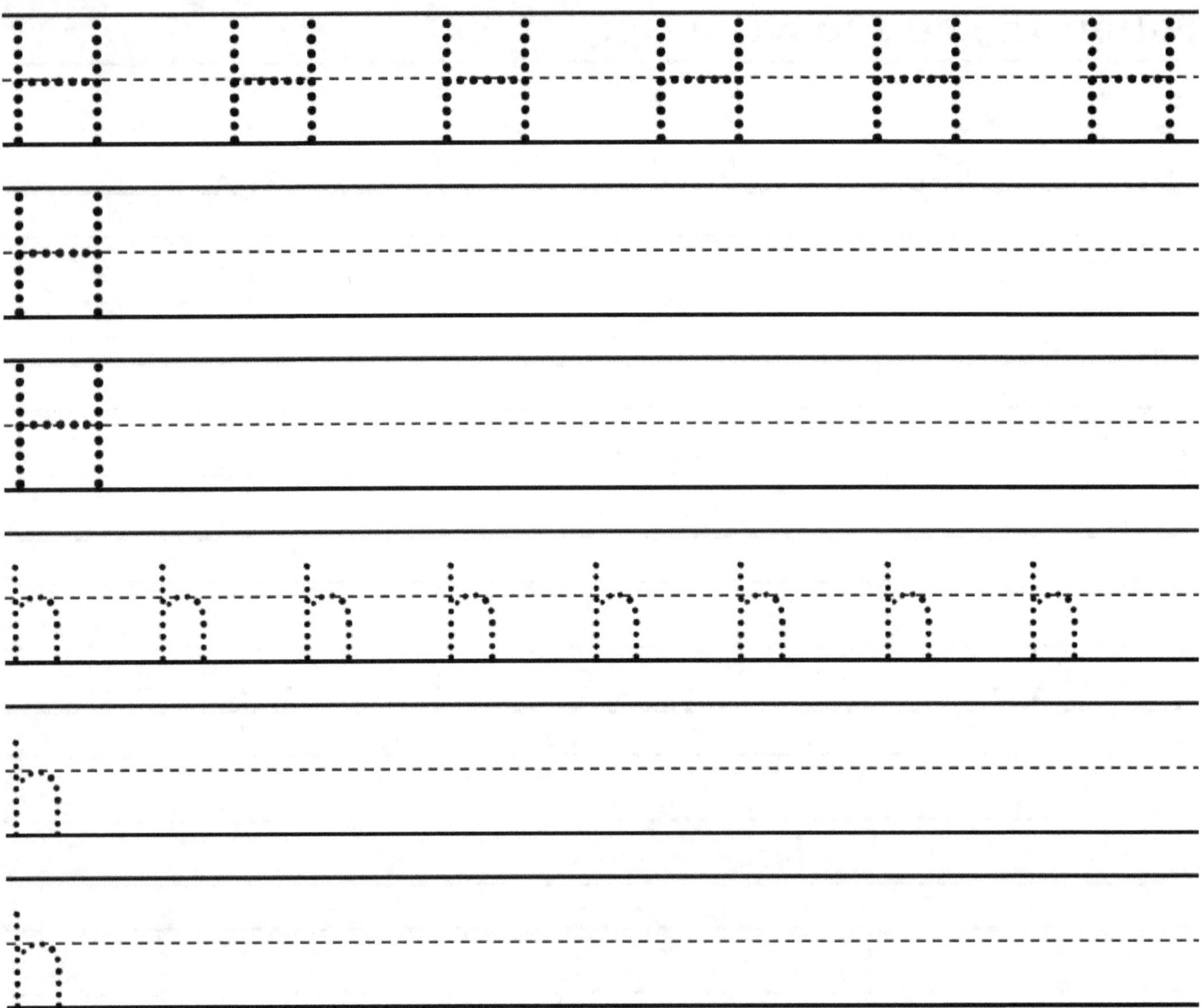

Words starting with the letter H:

→ Hippopotamus – Hippopotamus is a mammal.
→ Happy – I'm happy with my family.
→ Hungary – Hungary is a country.

Ii

Follow the dots to write Ii:

Words starting with the letter I:

→ Iguana – Iguana is a reptile.
→ Irritated – I'm irritated with his pranks.
→ India – India is a country.

Jj

Follow the dots to write Jj:

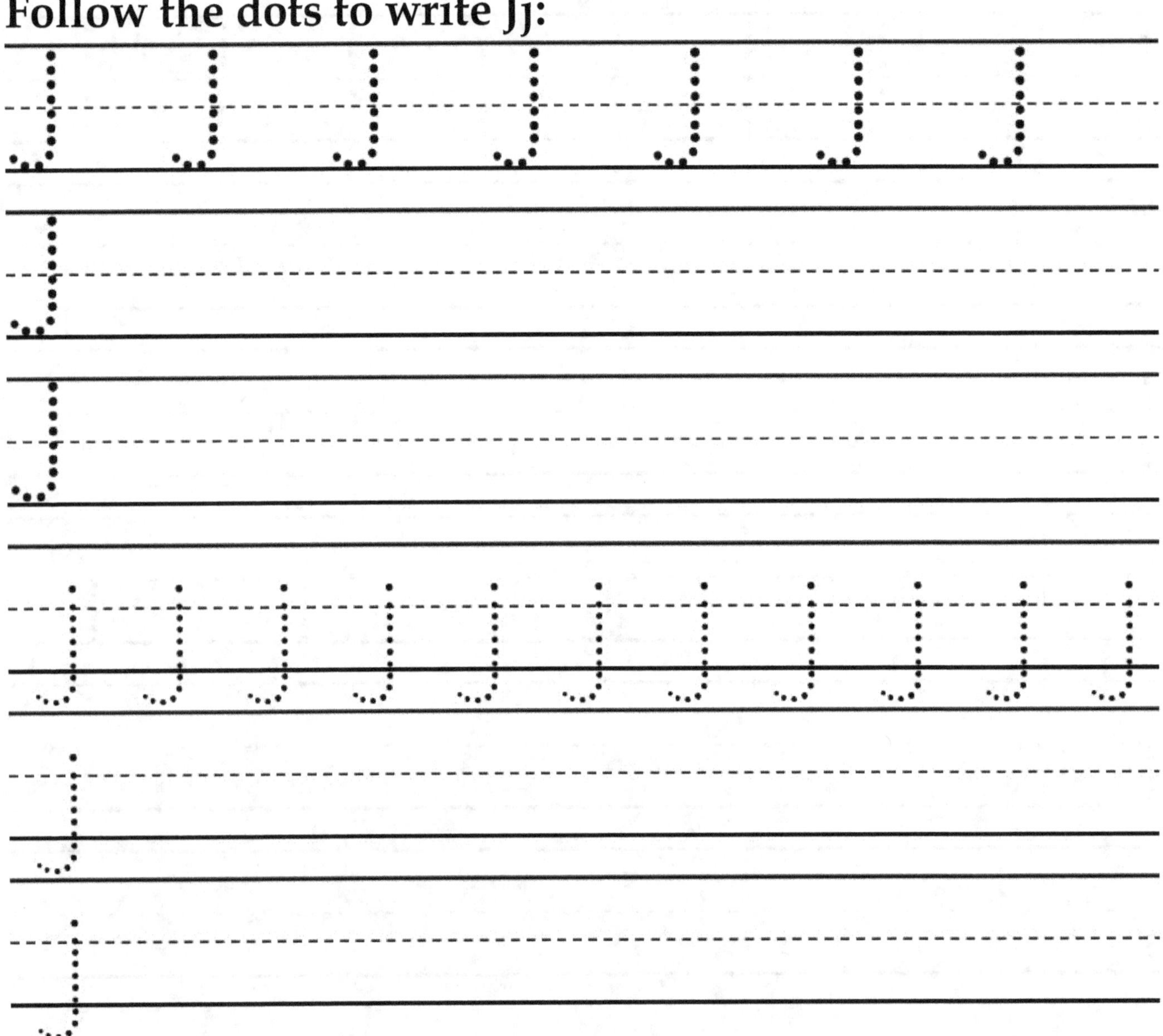

Words starting with the letter J:

➔ Jaguar – Jaguar is an animal.
➔ Joyful – I love joyful music.
➔ Japan – Japan is a country.

Kk

Follow the dots to write Kk:

Words starting with the letter K:

➔ Kangaroo – Kangaroo moves by hopping
➔ Kind – I am kind to my siblings.
➔ Kenya – Kenya is a country.

Ll

Follow the dots to write Ll:

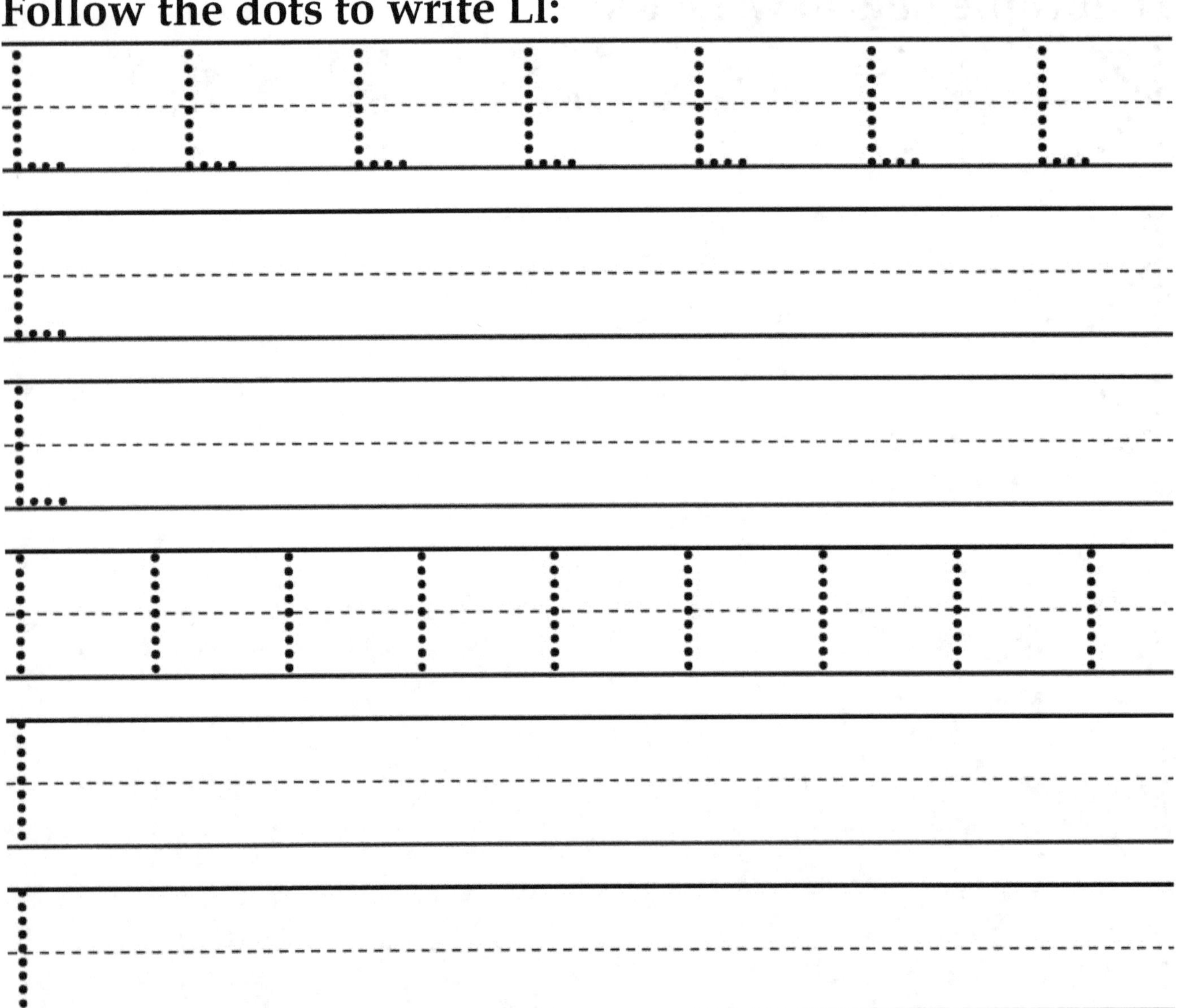

Words starting with the letter L:

➔ Ladybug – Ladybug is an insect.
➔ Love – I love my family.
➔ Laos – Laos is a country.

Mm

Follow the dots to write Mm:

Words starting with the letter M:

➔ Manatee – Manatee is a marine mammal.
➔ Mischievous – Being a mischievous child is not right.
➔ Malaysia – Malaysia is a country.

Nn

Follow the dots to write Nn:

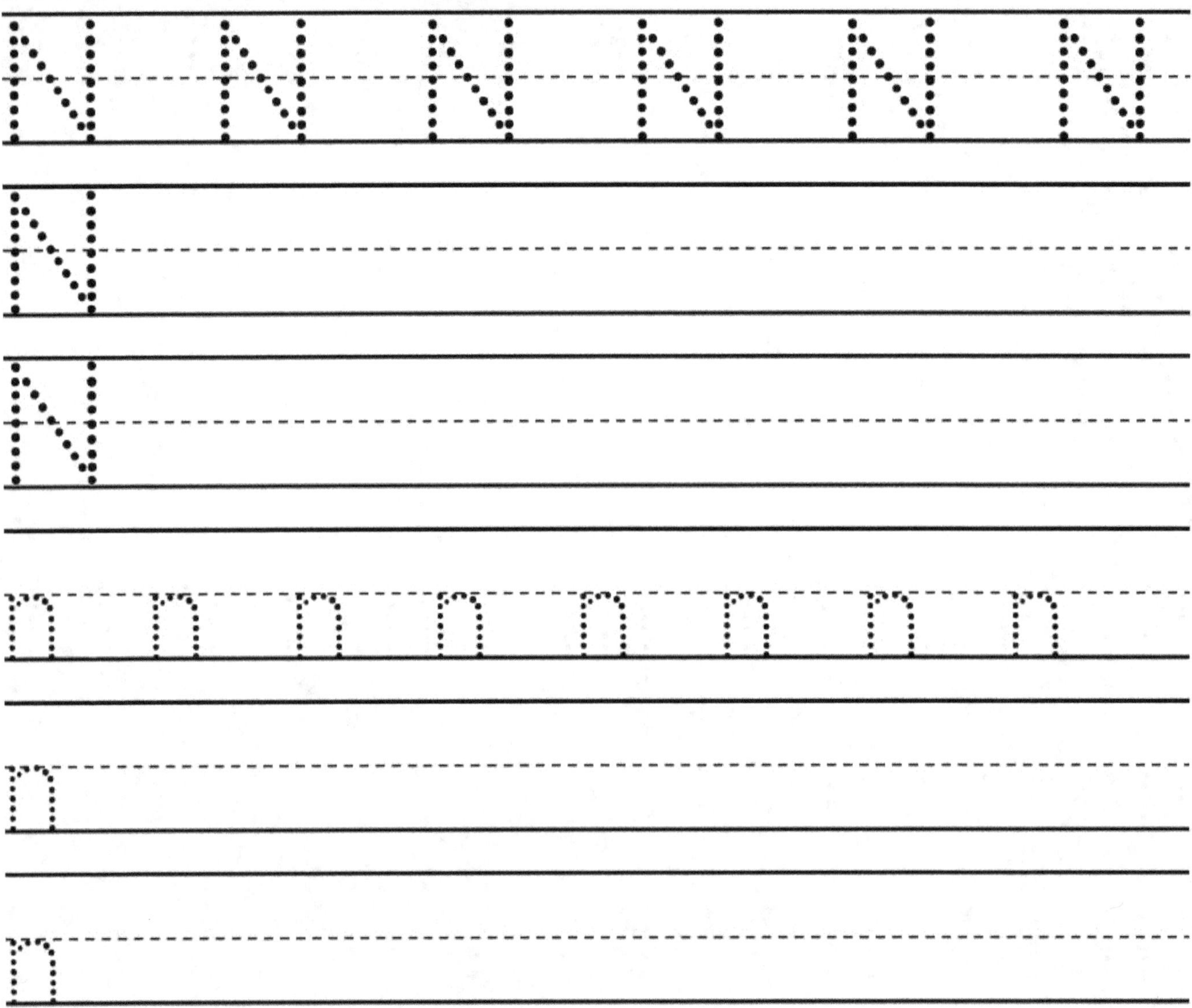

Words starting with the letter N:

➔ Nightingale – Nightingale is a passerine bird.
➔ Naughty – I am not a naughty child.
➔ New Zealand – New Zealand is a country.

Oo

Follow the dots to write Oo:

Words starting with the letter O:

➔ Octopus – Octopus is an eight-limbed seafood.
➔ Outstanding – I am an outstanding student.
➔ Oman – Oman is a country.

Pp

Follow the dots to write Pp:

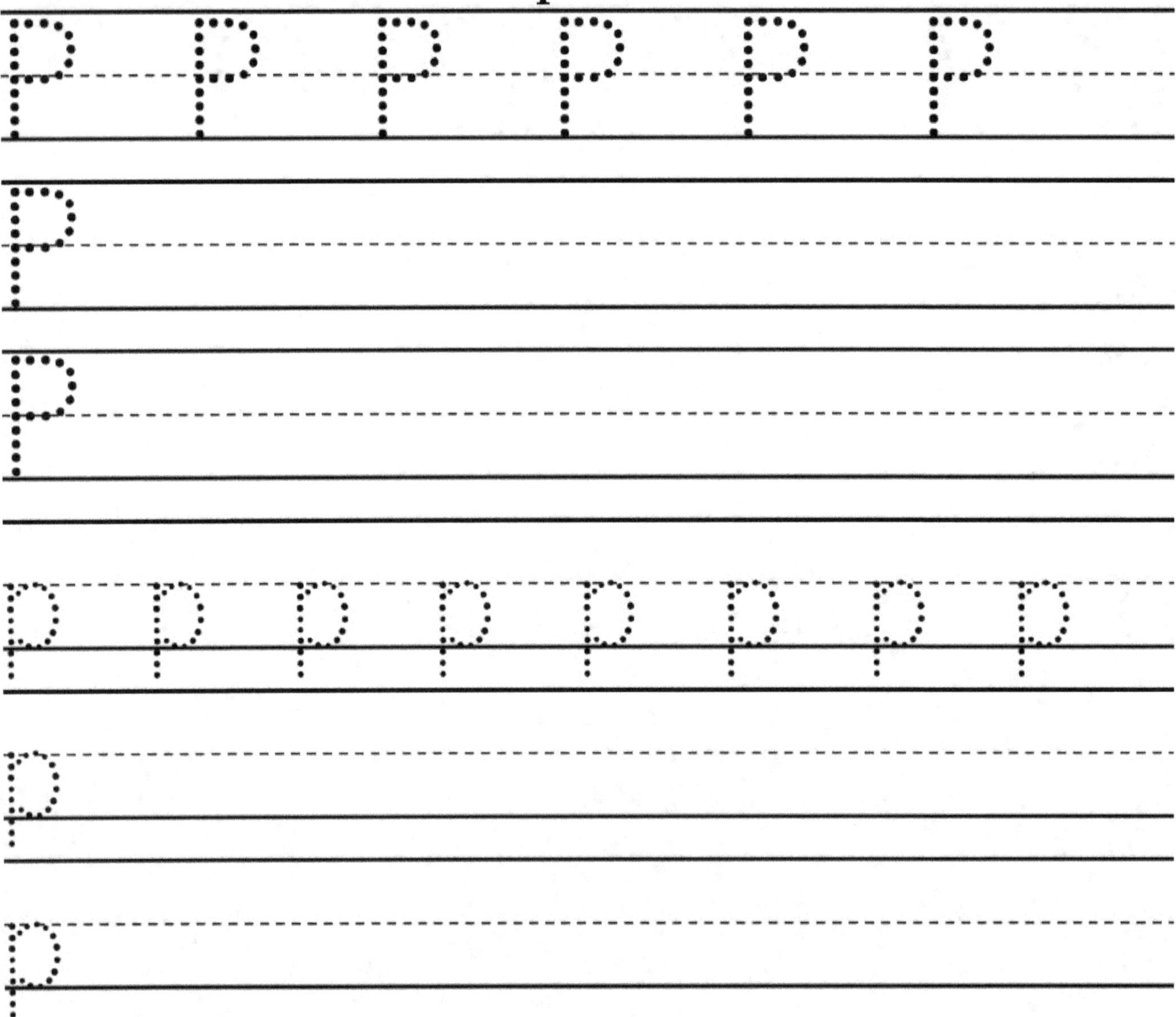

Words starting with the letter P:

➔ Peacock – Peacock display its tail to attract peahen.
➔ Pride – I take pride in what I do.
➔ Poland – Poland is a country.

Qq

Follow the dots to write Qq:

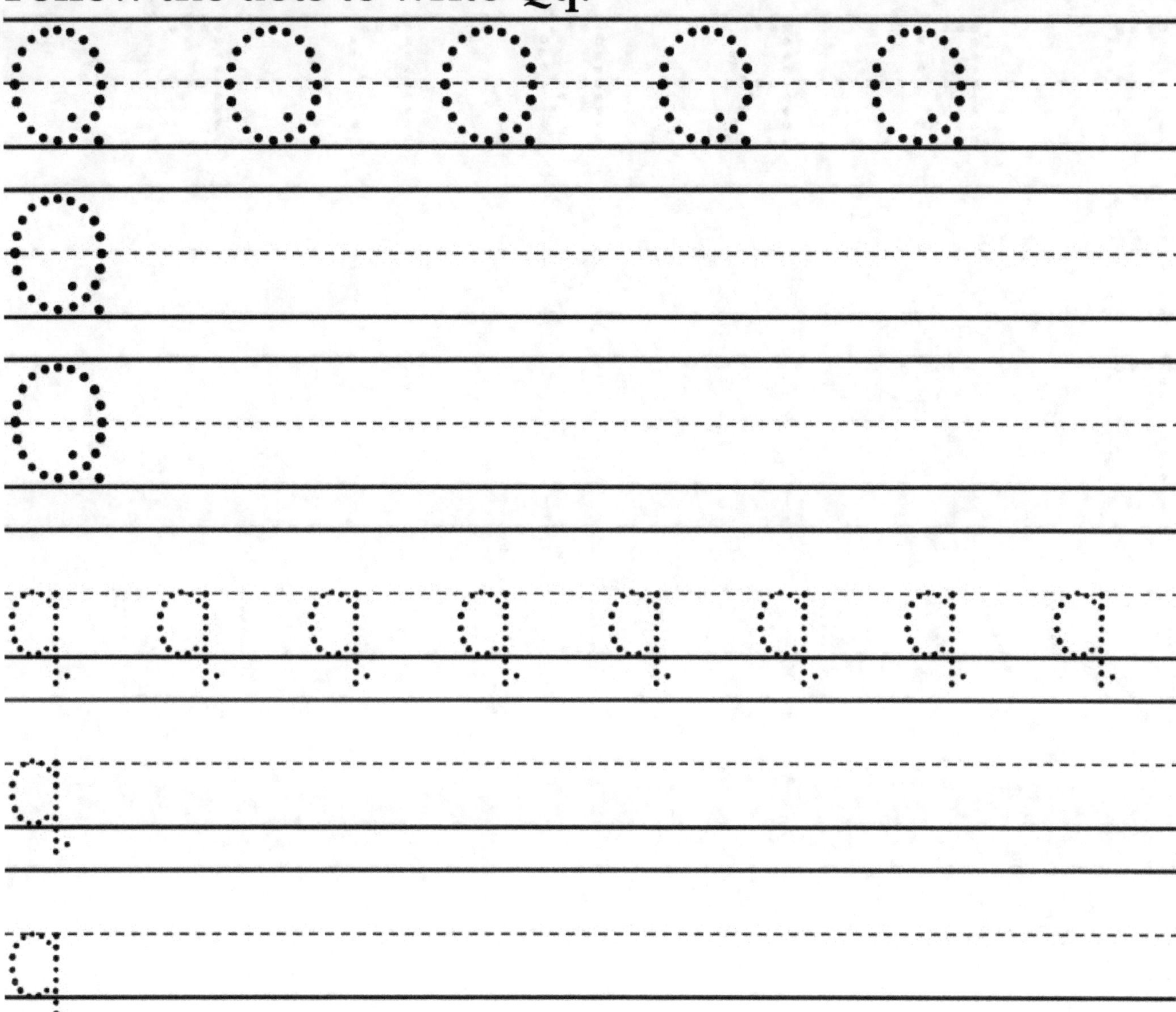

Words starting with the letter Q:

➔ Quail – Quail is a bird.
➔ Quiet – I keep quiet when teacher is teaching.
➔ Qatar – Qatar is a country.

Rr

Follow the dots to write Rr:

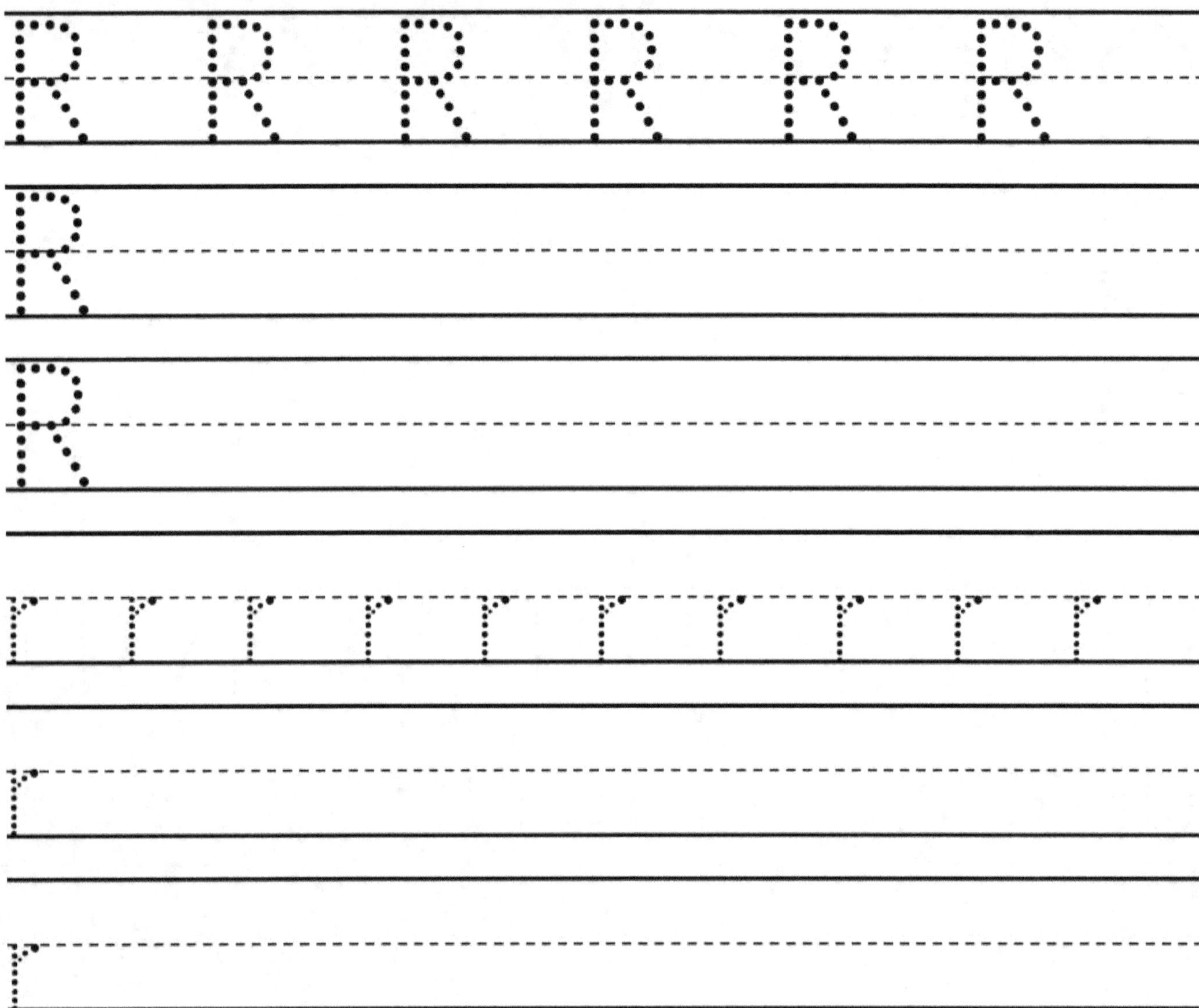

Words starting with the letter R:

➔ Rhinoceros – Rhinoceros is an animal.
➔ Respect – I respect my teacher.
➔ Russia – Russia is a country.

Ss

Follow the dots to write Ss:

Words starting with the letter S:

➔ Snakes – Snakes were hatch from eggs.
➔ Sincere – I am sincere to my best friend.
➔ Singapore – Singapore is a country.

Tt

Follow the dots to write Tt:

Words starting with the letter T:

➔ Tiger – Tiger is an apex predator.
➔ Thankful – I am thankful to my parents.
➔ Thailand – Thailand is a country.

Uu

Follow the dots to write Uu:

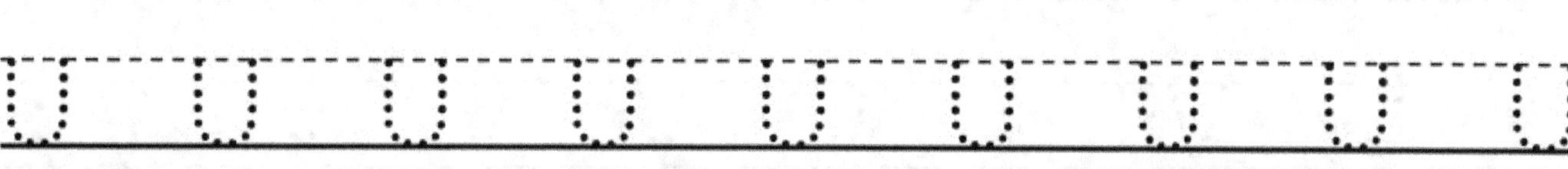

Words starting with the letter U:

➔ Uakari – Uakari is a primate.
➔ Unique – I am unique to my parents.
➔ United States – United States is a country.

Vv

Follow the dots to write Vv:

Words starting with the letter V:

→ Vampire Bat – Vampire Bat can fly.
→ Valiant – I am valiant.
→ Vietnam – Vietnam is a country.

Ww

Follow the dots to write Ww:

Words starting with the letter W:

➜ Whale – Whale is a marine mammal.
➜ Wisdom – I have wisdom.
➜ West Africa – West Africa is a region.

Xx

Follow the dots to write Xx:

Words starting with the letter X:

- → Xerus – Xerus is a rodent.
- → Xenial – I am being xenial in a party.
- → Xiamen – Xiamen is a city in China.

Yy

Follow the dots to write Yy:

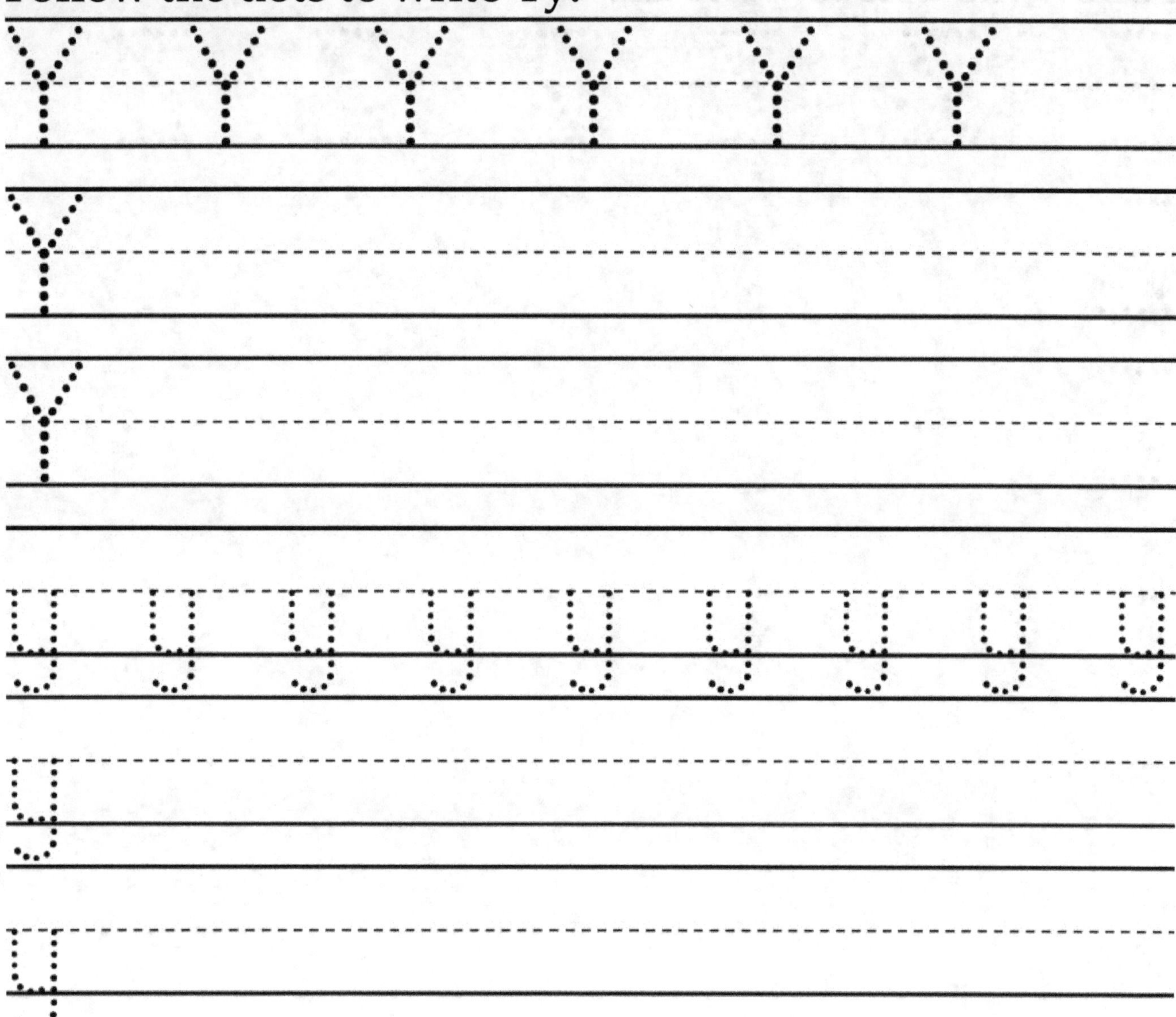

Words starting with the letter Y:

- ➜ Yak – Yak is an ox.
- ➜ Youthful – I am youthful.
- ➜ Yemen – Yemen is a country.

Zz

Follow the dots to write Zz:

Words starting with the letter Z:

→ Zebra – Zebra is an animal.
→ Zestful – Most successful people are zestful.
→ Zimbabwe – Zimbabwe is a country.

Start Writing Numbers 1-10

One (1)

Follow the dots to write:

One Sun

Two (2)

Follow the dots to write:

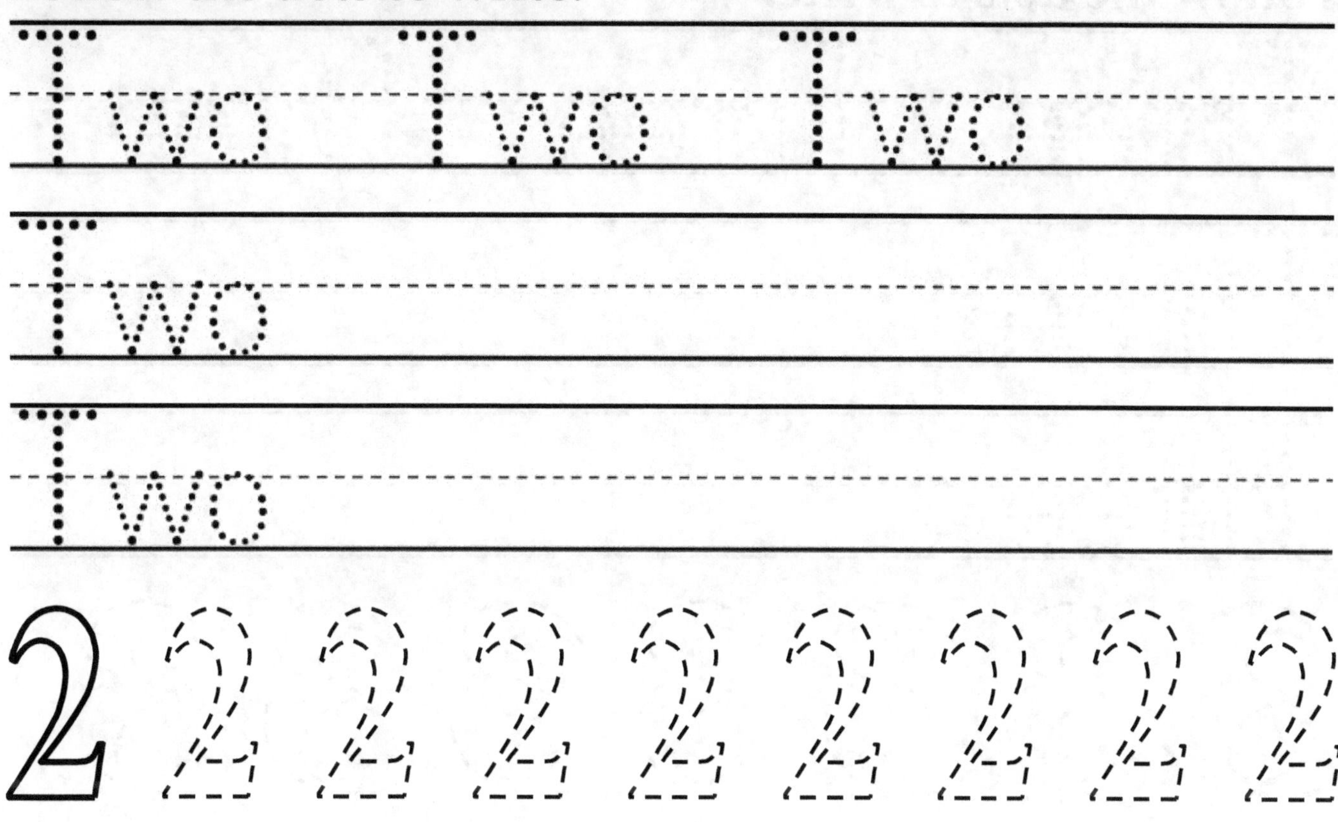

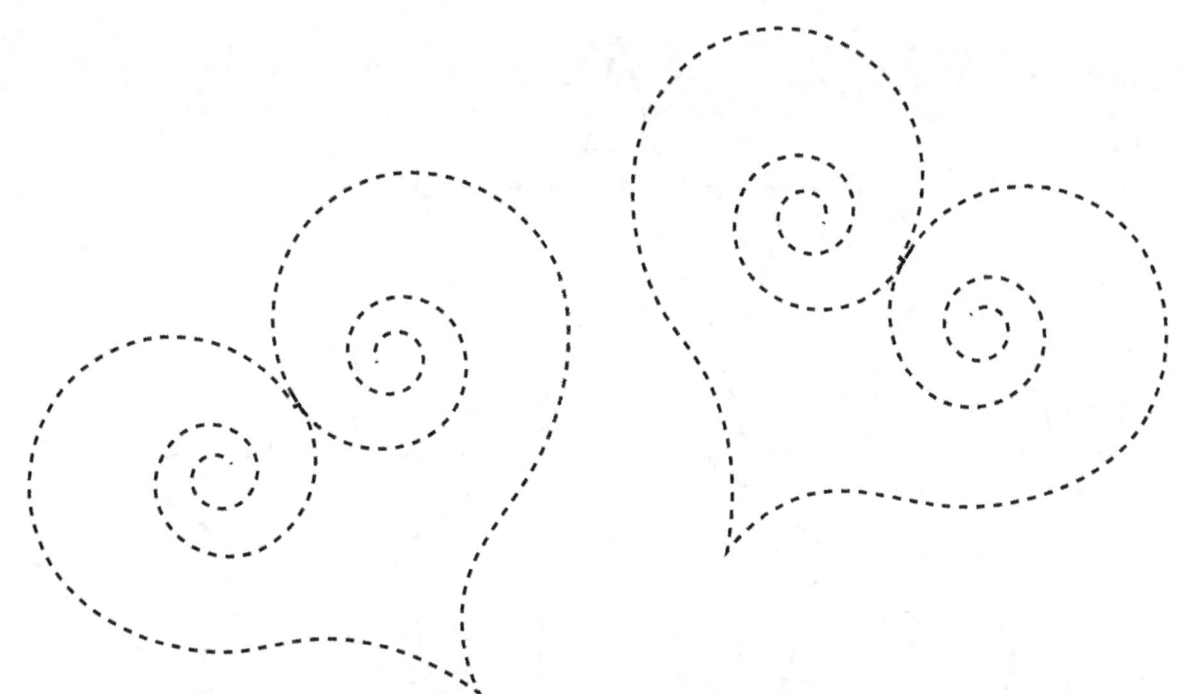

Two Hearts

Three (3)

Follow the dots to write:

Three Stars

Four (4)

Follow the dots to write:

Four Four Four

Four

Four

4 4 4 4 4 4 4 4 4

Four Monkeys

Five (5)

Follow the dots to write:

Five   Five   Five   Five

Five

Five

5 5 5 5 5 5 5 5 5 5

Five Paws

Six (6)

Follow the dots to write:

Six   Six   Six   Six

Six

Six

6 6 6 6 6 6 6 6 6 6 6

Six Smiley Face

Seven (7)

Follow the dots to write:

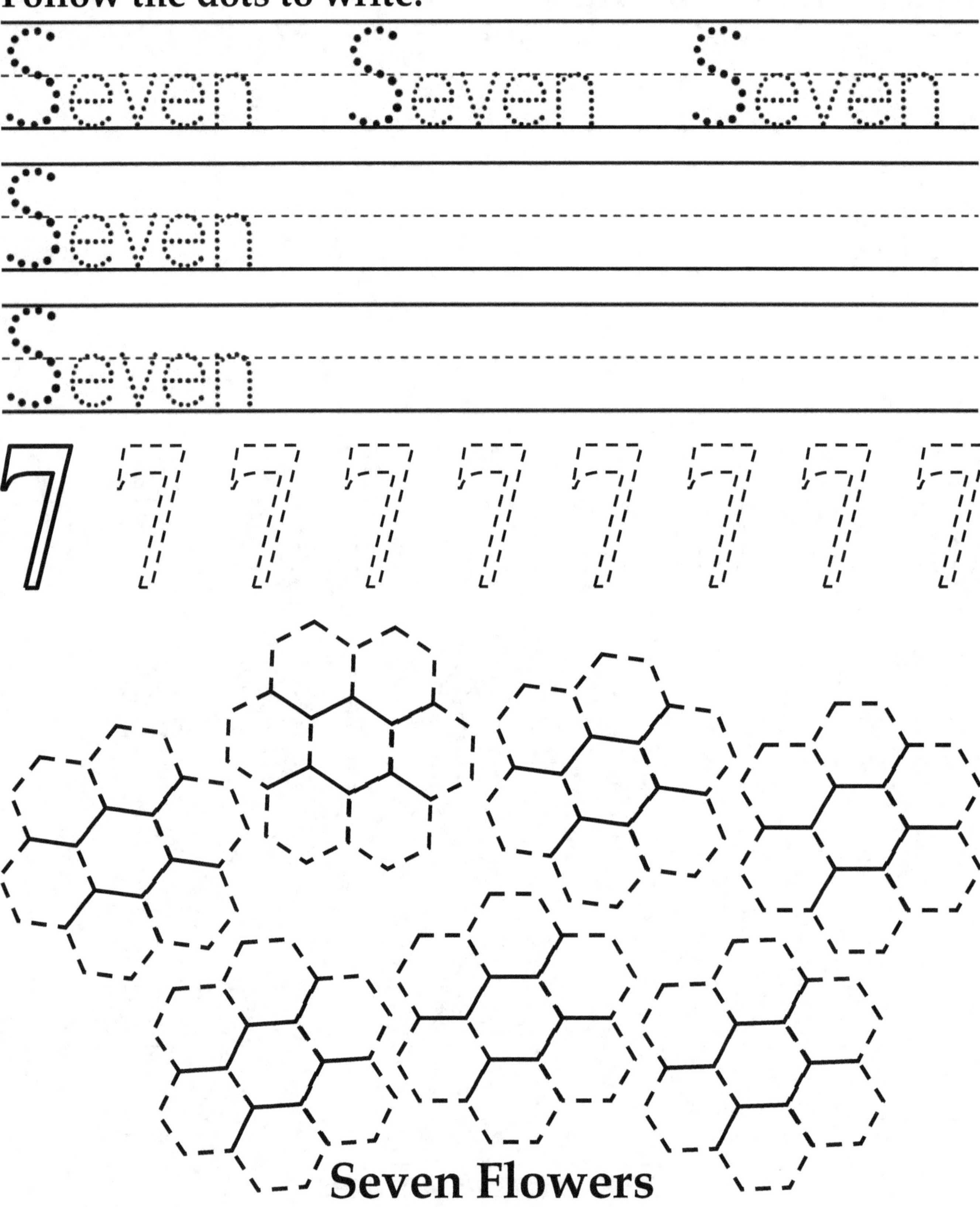

Seven Flowers

Eight (8)

Follow the dots to write:

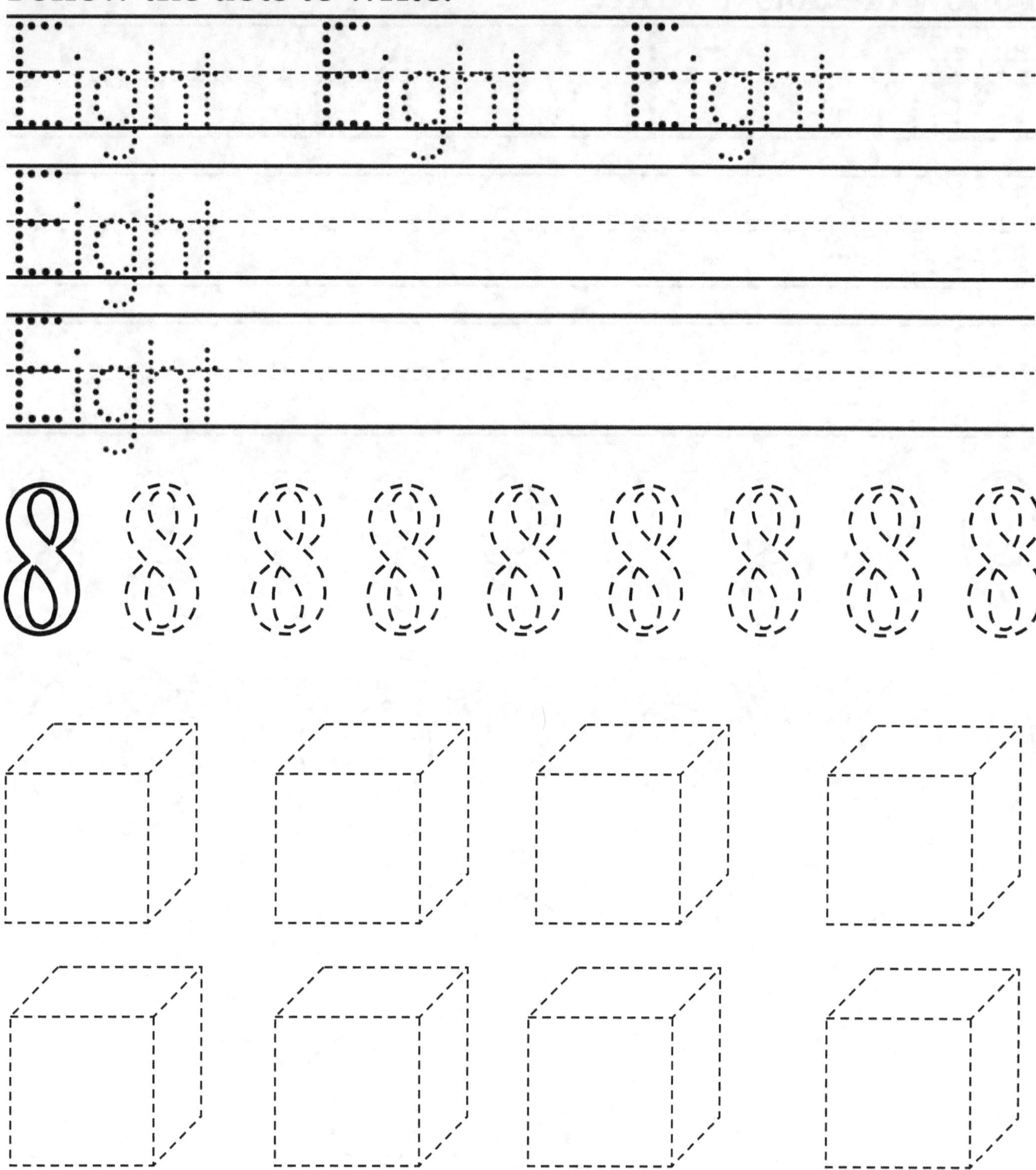

Eight Cubes

Nine (9)

Follow the dots to write:

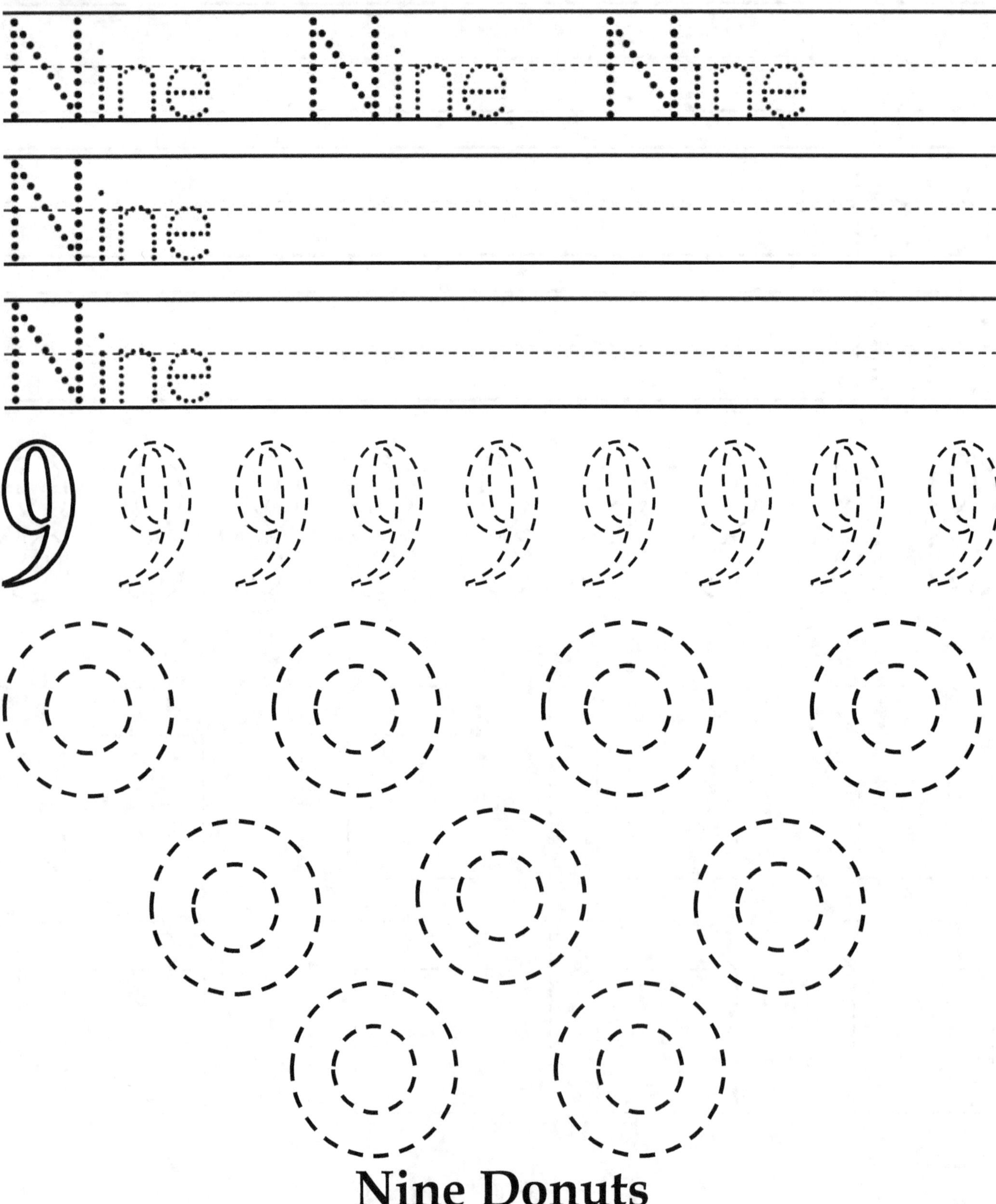

Nine Donuts

Ten (10)

Follow the dots to write:

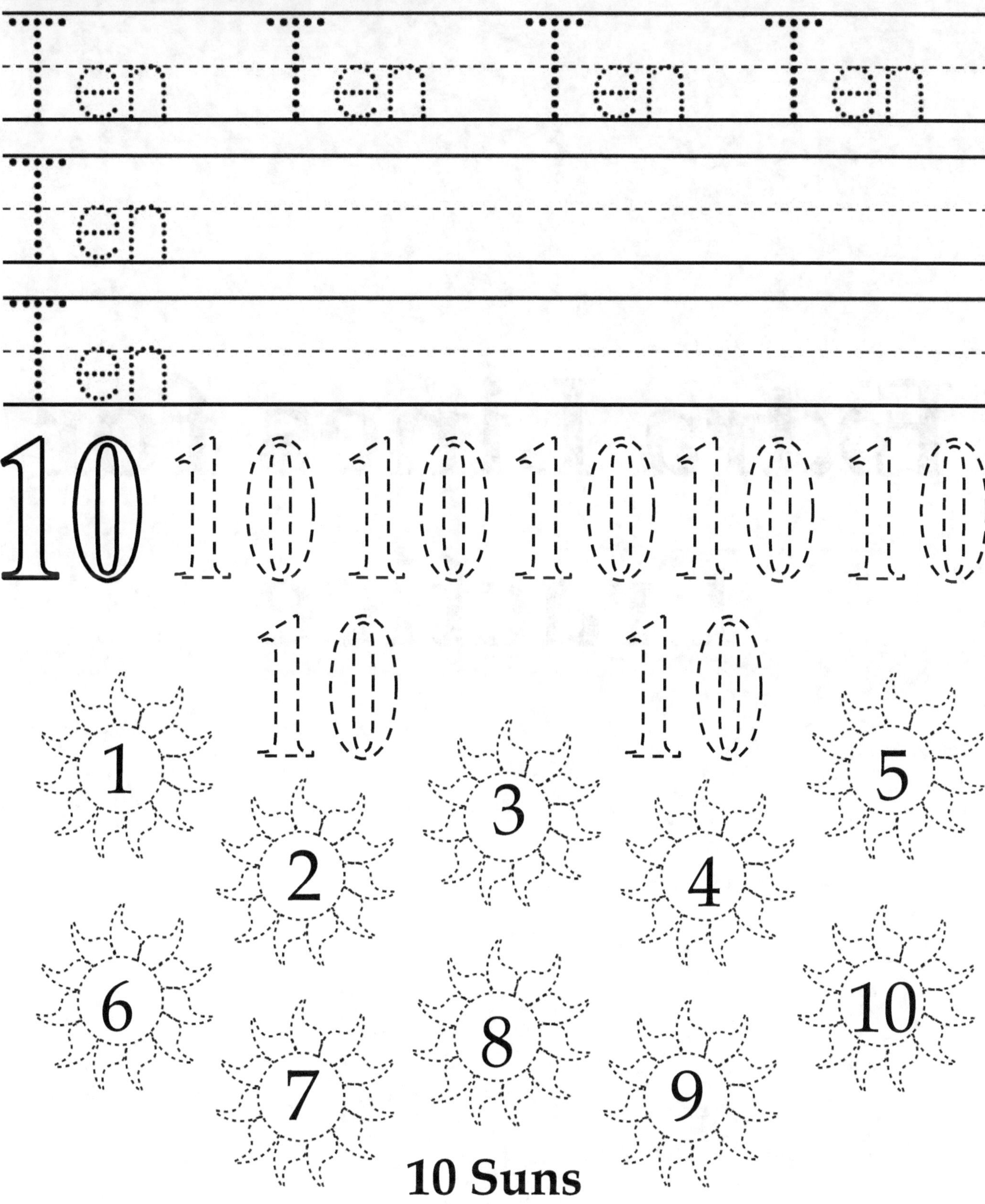

10 Suns

Extra Lines for Practice

~End of the Book~